TELL ME WHY
NIGHTS ARE LONESOME

Muriel Gold

Shoreline

© Muriel Gold, 2004
murielgoldpoole@videotron.ca   http://pages.infinit.net//murielgp
Cover design by Sarah Robinson
Sheet music, "Tell Me Why Nights are Lonesome," by Lee S. Roberts, 1917
Photographs from the collection of the author
Edited by Hana Askren
Printed in Canada by AGMV Marquis

Dépôt legal: National Library of Canada
et la Bibliothèque nationale du Québec

Published by Shoreline, 23 Ste-Anne, Ste-Anne-de-Bellevue, Quebec,
Canada H9X 1L1, 514-457-5733
shoreline@sympatico.ca   www.shorelinepress.ca

Second printing, fall 2004

National Library of Canada Cataloguing in Publication

Gold, Muriel

Tell me why nights are lonesome / Muriel Gold .
Includes bibliographical references and index.
ISBN 1-896754-35-X

1. Haltrecht, S. Bernard. 2. Haltrecht, Dora Ratner. 3. Montréal (Quebec)—
Biography. 4. Jews—Quebec (Province)—Montréal—Biography. I. Title.

FC2947.26.H34P66 2004 971.4'28 C2004-902660-7

For Geoffrey and Kenneth, Joshua, Vanessa, and Aleksa

Julien and Brigitte, Jared, Jessica, and Elizabeth

and

In loving memory of Dora and Bernard

ACKNOWLEDGMENTS

To my friends, relatives, and colleagues who pressed me with offers to read all or parts of the manuscript at various stages of its development: Carolann Butler, Barbara Burman, Glenn Gold, Stanley Haltrecht, Merle Haltrecht Matte, Alexandre Hausvater, Robert Lecker, Beverley Mitchell, Robert Robinson, Johanne Schumann (in particular), William Weintraub, and Jack Zolov.

To archivists: Stewart Renfrew, Queen's University, and Nadine Small, University of Saskatchewan. To librarians: Nancy Lemon, Queen's University and Ronald Finegold, Jewish Public Library, Montreal, and to Janice Rosen, Canadian Jewish Congress.

To Ted Friedgut for supplying information about his family.

To Allan Putterman, for taking the trouble to photograph our family's houses.

To Erica and Warren, Glenn and Hedda, Christopher and Carolann, Betsy and Mary for their friendship and love.

To my husband, Ronald Poole, for his unqualified love, constant support, and computer skills.

To Sarah Robinson, graphic artist, whose creativity is self-evident.

To Hana Askren, my editor at Shoreline, whose care and insight helped to clarify and fine-tune the manuscript.

And especially, to publisher Judith Isherwood of Shoreline, who found the story "a slice of history that should be preserved."

CONTENTS

All-in-One Tree of Salek Bernard Haltrecht

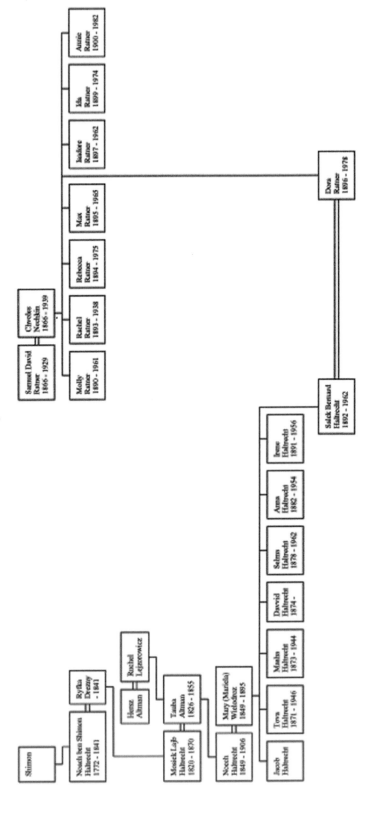

Descendants of Salek Bernard Haltrecht

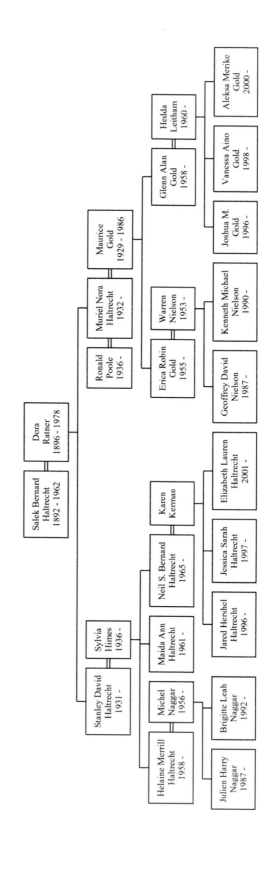

...when I look into the eyes of my children, I see my own immortality. They will continue my existence long after I shall have passed into the great and unknown beyond. It is in this phenomenon that we can unveil the true secret of the parents' intense feelings for their offspring. They are the flesh of our flesh, the blood of our blood, and the spirit of our spirit.

from S.B. Haltrecht's Bar Mitzvah speech to his son, Stanley, 1944

To my dear Miss D. Ratner

A FAREWELL

Good-bye,
Farewell, I bid thee, farewell.
I hear the sacred ring
Of the golden bell:
The very sad ding-ding.

I will always pray and avow
That angels might keep thee, guide,
Bless and watch; for thou
Art Nature's greatest pride.

Sweet soul, think of me
With kind thoughts of him who hath
Not sufficient words for thee
To express with his breath.

Please, I pray thee, remember me,
For this I now warm tears do shed.
I shall never, no never forget thee,
Nay, not even on my death-bed.

Salek Bernard Haltrecht

The young man writing this gallant poem filled with devotion to his seventeen-year old sweetheart will one day become my father, Bernard. And the teen-age girl to whom he professes his love will be my mother, Dora. From the poem, brimming with sentimentality and unabashed passion, one might deduce that Bernard is taking leave of the country, or, heaven forbid, the world! In actual fact, he is returning to Regina, Saskatchewan from a visit to Montreal, Quebec.

PROLOGUE

Some time after my father's death, my mother decided to sell her home and move to an apartment. I went over to help her organize the move. Dozens of items had accumulated, most forgotten for many years. What to discard? What to keep? In the furnished basement there was a built-in upholstered bench with a lid. A variety of items had been stored inside. My eyes fell on a scruffy, dusty, old shoe box, tearing at the edges. I blew off the dust and removed the lid. It was full of letters, letters addressed to Miss Dora Ratner in my father's handwriting, letters addressed to Mr. S. B. Haltrecht in my mother's handwriting.

I did not know then what I would do with these letters. But I did know they were precious and had to be saved. So, with my mother's permission, I carried them home and eagerly read them, then carefully replaced them in the box, and deposited them on the top shelf in my den cupboard for some unknown future use.

It would be a long time before I would tell my parents' story, the story of two young people from different countries who serendipitously met, were attracted to one another, and corresponded across the vastness of Canada over an eight-year period. It was an era in which courtship was distinctly different from the way it is today. Their correspondence spanned major socio-political world events: the Russian Revolution, the first World War, the rise of the Third Reich, the flu epidemic, the suffragette movement, the beginnings of Zionism. Their letters, reflecting all these topics as well as the theatrical and cultural events of their day, were a reflection of Canadian history.

A few years ago I was approached by a colleague, Barbara MacKay, a drama therapist, and asked to collaborate on a theatre project. Her idea was to organize five women in the drama field to put together a collective creation based upon our relationships with our mothers and grandmothers, and to present the piece at the forthcoming Drama Therapy Conference in San Francisco. Each woman would dramatize her own story, emerging themes would be integrated and accompanying music and sound effects would heighten the drama.

Always keen to be involved in creative experiences, I tentatively agreed to participate. Tentatively because I was doubtful whether my contribution would be of interest. After all, it was my father who was the dynamic high achiever in the family. It was he who had the persistence to succeed on his own in a foreign country. It was he who was highly educated, highly motivated and well loved. It was he who had recorded his roots dating back to the mid-eighteenth century. Of my mother's roots I knew nothing. My connection was always stronger to my father. As for grandmothers, I never knew mine.

Barbara and I travelled to Toronto to meet with the three others. We talked and talked, telling each other in turn something of our connections to our mothers and grandmothers.

When my turn came, I spoke of my mother and her sisters - how the whole family had arrived in Montreal from Russia in 1908 when my mother was 12 years old, how they had all studied piano and voice with an internationally renowned pianist and his wife, a singing teacher - and that one of my aunts, an early feminist, was a member of the revolutionary underground in Russia. I told of how in Montreal this same aunt founded the Montreal Dental Assistants Association and that the two youngest aunts were among the first Jewish girls to graduate from Macdonald College to become teachers. I continued saying that they were the first Jewish family to live in a highly desirable French-Canadian neighbourhood and that my mother was the first Jewish girl to work in the offices of the Grand Trunk Railway, which later became the Canadian National Railways. And on and on.

I mentioned that my mother met my father when she was sixteen on his stopover from London, England to Saskatchewan. I said that it was the commencement of a long-distance romance that lasted eight years. I admitted that I had many of those letters in my possession. I explained that although I did not know my grandmothers, I did have a very close relationship with my devoted aunts, my mother's sisters.

To my surprise, the others listened intently and seemed engrossed in what I thought was an ordinary story. What impressed me most was a comment made by one of the group. "This is so fascinating. You don't know how lucky you are," she said. "To have come from parents who had a long-distance love affair that spanned eight years, to have lived in a house where there was a loving relationship, and to have documents in your possession as memorabilia. I am honestly quite jealous. My parents married after knowing each other three weeks and fought throughout their married life. Their noisy arguments are my childhood memories."

The next day I took the train home to Montreal. Upon reaching my apartment, I took the box containing the letters from the shelf in my cupboard. The letters were all in sequence as originally organized. Attempting impartiality, I extracted my mother's letters, relegating my father's letters back to the box.

I discovered that teen-aged Dora was well read, culturally active, read and wrote her third language, English, perfectly, and studied a fourth language in order to feel at home with her French-Canadian neighbours. She took courses in singing and piano and studied part time at McGill University. All of these were extra-curricular activities. During the day she worked as a stenographer for a national corporation, comfortably blending in with gentile co-workers.

A story began to emerge, not just of one person, but of two young people, both immigrants to Canada in their youth, and of their assimilation in the new country, their hopes, their dreams, the obstacles in their path, and their developing love for one another.

Shortly after my father's death, a colleague of his, David Rome, national archivist at the Canadian Jewish Congress, offered to collaborate with me on a book about my father. I should have undertaken the task then, and written about my father, his roots, his struggle for an education in Canada, how he fit into Canadian history, and his influence upon the Montreal Jewish community. But, devastated by his death, and unsure of myself as a writer at that time, I was not ready. Years later, with most of his colleagues gone, and without all the factual information about his life, I felt unequipped to write his biography. The closest I came was dedicating my first book to his memory.

My father, S. Bernard Haltrecht, died on August 11th, 1962. It was an immense loss to all who knew him and particularly to our nuclear family. Not long afterwards, I wrote some poetry in his memory. A couple of the poems were published in *The Jewish Spectator,* a New York literary journal, in the fall of 1969. One of them was inspired by the last night of his life when he was in a coma, and while I sat beside his bed holding his hand, I heard him pleading with God to "Give us back the six million Jews." I was touched and surprised by this comment because my father was not a survivor, nor was he particularly religious. I surmised that the magnitude of the Holocaust is so imprinted on the Jewish soul and conscience that perhaps to be Jewish is to bear this sorrow in our subconscious thoughts. I know that the first time I saw a Holocaust film and saw young naked children taken off to the camps, I bore their humiliation and thought, "There but for the grace of God go I."

AUSCHWITZ

if you looked closely
into his eyes
you could see
pools of people
drowning.

He carried the bones of Auschwitz
in his head,
and on his shoulders
their children,
but his hands
he kept free

On the anniversary of my father's death from colon cancer, my mother suggested I light a yahrzeit candle in his memory. What harm could it do? So I bought one, placed it on the kitchen table, and lit it. Unexpectedly the experience inspired the following poem.

THEY SAID

They said
I should light a candle
in your memory
so I did
not wishing to offend
the God of my people

I did not know
that the flame
would remind me
of the flecks in your eyes
when you reflected
as you so often did

I

THE MEETING AND THE COURTSHIP

1 ✡ BERNARD

Salek Bernard Haltrecht was born in the picturesque town of Plock (pronounced "Plotsk"), Poland, on August 21st, 1892. The town, then part of the old Russian Empire, bordered Poland's winding main river artery, the Vistula. Its steep banks, crowned by the splendid ancient walls of the town, were a vision of beauty. One of Poland's smaller provincial cities, Plock was situated a hundred kilometres west of Warsaw. At the turn of the 20th century the city of Plock had a population of 50,000, of whom 35,000 were Jewish. The youngster, known to his family as Sallie, spoke Yiddish at home, learned Russian in school, spoke Hebrew in *cheder,* and Polish on the streets.

Unlike the ghetto Jews still existing in medieval fashion with their black cloaks, their long beards and their curly locks hanging from their temples, the Haltrecht family lived a more modern religious existence and were avid readers of books in a variety of fields such as politics, social history, and literature. Also unlike the Russian Jewish emigrants who had been pouring into Poland during the nineteenth century to escape the barbarous persecution by the Czarist Government, the Haltrecht family had lived in Poland for generations. They were able to trace their roots to the mid-1700s when their ancestor, Rabbi Noah, had been officially given the Haltrecht name, meaning "keep right," in recognition of his communal activities and his outstanding scholarship as a high-profile Rabbinical judge. His book, *Toldas Noah,* meaning "The Generations of Noah," recorded not only his sermons, but also the hundreds of letters he wrote to the government on behalf of his community's welfare.

Sallie's father, Noah (Noach), had married his childhood sweetheart, Mary (Mariela) Wieledrus, in 1869 when they were both 19 years old. She bore him five girls: Tova, Masha, Selma, Anna, Irene - and three boys: Jacob, David, and Salek. She gave birth to her youngest child, Salek, when she was 42 years old, and three years later, became ill and died.

MARY AND NOAH

Typical of children who are the youngest in large families, Sallie grew up fast. Although Noah, his father, had remarried soon after his wife's death, this second wife did not turn out to be an ideal parent. She was distant - perhaps overwhelmed by her newly acquired domestic duties. Noah was disappointed that she and the children could not bond with one another and he tried to compensate for her lack of warmth by spending as much time with his family as he could spare from his duties at the synagogue.

Noah was particularly concerned about the two youngest children, Irene and Sallie, and most particularly about Sallie. He was the baby in the family and Mary had doted on him. He was used to being cuddled and given special treats, and the older sisters now tried to compensate for their stepmother's lack of affection. Every night before going to sleep, they noticed he would hum a song to himself that their mother used to sing. He confessed to his older sister, Selma, that he talked to his mama at night and told her his secrets. He said that when he squeezed his eyes really tight, he could see her standing by his bedroom door. She always smiled at him, came to his bed, and tucked him under the covers. In his adulthood, Sallie said he retained the image of his "real" mother throughout his entire life.

Most of Sallie's daytime was occupied with school and *cheder* and with his reading. In 1896, the first Jewish Public Library was established in Plock and Sallie took full advantage of it. He loved books and read voraciously. Noah constantly reminded his children of their noble Jewish heritage and saw to it that a climate of learning was maintained in their home. To his sons in particular he emphasized their obligation to emulate the standards passed on to them by their ancestor and his namesake, the famous Rabbinical judge. But it was obvious that it would be his youngest son who had the most potential. He was always poring over books, and his understanding of adult material in diverse areas such as geography, history and literature was remarkable. Following some of his older siblings' examples, he attended a variety of literary and political lectures delivered by local and visiting intellectual speakers. His father was not surprised that at the "gymnasium" which his young son attended, the teachers reported that Sallie was far ahead of his classmates in most subjects.

Father and son would spend long hours together in discussions ranging from school subjects to mysticism and current events. This boy revelled in discussion and argumentation. Normally a reserved person, Noah could not refrain from boasting to close friends and family about his son's intellect, inquisitive mind, and endearing personality. He even let Sallie know that he envisioned a great future for him. With such intellectual stimulation and loving personal regard, it was no wonder Sallie treasured their special time together.

But one chilly morning in April, 1906, Sallie awoke to sounds of commotion. He jumped out of bed and raced to the kitchen where his sisters, Masha and Irene, sat, heads in hands, sobbing. The father he adored had suffered a heart attack in his sleep and died instantly. He was only 56 years old.

Over the following weeks, as Sallie recovered from the shock, he realized there was not much to keep him from leaving Plock. He felt no deep ties to his stepmother, and it was clear that the possibilities of a "great future" lay neither in the town of Plock nor in anti-Semitic Eastern Europe. Sallie, only 13 years of age, thought that under the present circumstances, he should move on to a larger world and a freer environment. Five older siblings had already moved overseas -

Selma to Hamburg; Jacob, Tova, and Anna to London; and David to Berlin. Sallie chose London, with a stopover in Berlin.

The year before, the British government had introduced the Immigration Restriction Act, making it difficult for East European Jews to immigrate. Sallie would stay temporarily in Berlin while Anna and her husband, Edmond, pulled strings to enable him to join them in England.

David lived in Berlin with his wife, Elsa, and four small children. He had become a successful entrepreneur, the owner of a thriving tobacco factory and two stores. The adolescent boy from Plock was exposed to his brother's prosperous and privileged existence - a rich cultural and intellectual life steeped in the arts, music in particular. Their lifestyle made a lasting impression on Sallie.

David pointed out with pride the lovely houses in the finest neighbourhoods where many Jewish families lived. He and Elsa took Bernard to the opera and the theatre, where they, and many of their Jewish friends, enjoyed the best seats. However, Bernard was to learn that there was a negative aspect to what appeared to be an enviable situation. Jewish affluence attracted attention and envy from many quarters of Christian society. Even though they were barred from a number of desired vocations and were excluded from high society, their cultural sophistication and wealth still incited open anti-Semitism.

Bernard stayed with his Berlin family in their elegant spacious home for several months, where he became proficient in yet another language. When the papers came through, he moved to be with his other siblings in London, England. His sister and brother-in-law, Anna and Edmond Frenkiel, were the most well-established. They lived in Oxford Street close by Mayfair, London's most fashionable district, where Edmond owned a language school. Anna and Edmond were living in an assimilated area of London, while Bernard's other relatives who had migrated to London lived in the Jewish East End. His eldest sister, Tova, had married in Poland when Bernard was four years old. Her husband was Menusha Maizels, a widower with a young son, Samuel.

Following the birth of two more children, Mary and Sadie, Tova and Menusha had left the country and travelled across Europe to Belgium where another child, Jerry, was born. Two years later, in 1903, they had immigrated to England and rented a large house in the very fashionable area of Brixton, South London. Their fourth child, Mark, was born in 1905, and three years later Tova and Menusha separated. Menusha stayed in the big house with the four children, and Tova kept three-year-old Mark. It is rumoured that in later years Tova had what we call today a "live-in boyfriend."

A number of cousins had opened businesses in Whitechapel, which was largely occupied by Jews from all over Europe. Two of Bernard's cousins owned "Haltrecht's," which grew into a clothing department store. It provided the families with a comfortable living for many years until 1940, when it disappeared in flames during the London Blitz (along with the portion of the Jewish East End deliberately destroyed by German bombers).

Despite relatives' offers of help, 14-year-old Bernard insisted on living alone and paying his own way. It was not unusual for boys that age to be taken out of school to earn a living but Bernard's circumstances were different from other boys his age. He had no parents and no home. In Poland he had been told by his teachers, by his friends and by his father, that he was intellectually mature for his age. Now he had to demonstrate that he was also emotionally mature. When he felt particularly lonesome he told himself it was an adventure, his first time living alone. For inspiration and comfort he thought back to his Bar Mitzvah when, with his father and the Rabbi beside him, he had been initiated into manhood. Now that his father was gone, he would make every effort to live up to his father's high expectations.

The residential streets were well supplied with modest rooming houses which would do for now. He didn't require much space. For the next six years, Bernard lived in London struggling to make ends meet. He worked long hours, first as a watchmaker's assistant, then as the watchmaker's bookkeeper. No matter how meagre his wages were, he managed to put a few farthings away each month. He avoided public transportation rain or shine, walking to every destination. He became expert at shopping frugally and borrowed books regularly from the Whitechapel Public Library. Most evenings he pored over English books in his attic by candlelight.

It was the reign of Edward VII, a monarch whose love of pageantry was a welcome reaction against the austerity of Victorianism. London was in transition from old to new. Horse-buses and motor-buses were seen on the roads. Hansoms and glittering new taxis competed for passengers. The Strand and Oxford Street were a mélange of past and present. Most businessmen went about in old silk toppers, but some modern chaps sported the new soft Stetson. Most women continued to wear trailing skirts that swept up the soot of the streets. Only the progressive non-conformists and the suffragettes were sensible enough to wear skirts hemmed two inches above the heel.

Meanwhile the suffragettes enlivened the streets with their parades and shenanigans. For Bernard, a young immigrant, seeing women chaining themselves to Parliament Square railings or hearing about them padlocking themselves to door handles of Ministers' private homes was awesome. Although he had not personally come across any women trained in ju-jitsu overthrowing policemen, he saw photographs and articles describing these incidents in the newspapers. Bernard was 15 years old on January 14, 1908, when Women's Suffrage was granted in Britain. Although they received much public ridicule, he secretly admired their courage, dedication, and persistence in their fight for equality, virtues which he vowed to emulate throughout his life.

Bernard was well settled in London in terms of family and friends, but the lack of opportunity for advancement and the appalling poverty in the city grated on him. There was a sharp contrast between the relative comfort of families in the West End and the manner in which the poverty-stricken working classes struggled in the East End, or so it seemed to Bernard. He passed a shop where barrels of herrings stood in a gloomy interior. A lick of herring and little else besides sustained many a family on the point of starvation. In this country, he noticed, with no fear of the knife, one could still be stifled in body and spirit.

Yet he was grateful. England had taken him in and at least there was no fear of pogrom. Not two years earlier, the streets of Kishinev, a city not far from Odessa, had run with blood during a three-day officially sanctioned massacre ferocious even by the Russian standard of pogroms. Almost nothing else was talked of amongst the Jews of Europe, who worried over where the knife would fall next. And fall it did in licensed butchery. Men could rape and pillage and kill, with no one to check them. At least in England life was safe.

Still, for Bernard, North America was the land of opportunity. A lover of history and geography and an insatiable reader from an early age, he had always digested information about other parts of the world. Canada, with its vast expanses of land and relatively few inhabitants, was inviting. The Western countryside sounded picturesque and romantic compared to the dusty, polluted streets of London. The country had been actively seeking settlers to clear and eventually cultivate these lands, and a number of farm colonies had already been formed.

He learned that the farmers in Western Canada had little or no access to quality education. From the intense Canadian advertising campaign overseas, he gleaned that there was an acute shortage of teachers in the West and that jobs were plentiful. Since he was not interested in farming per se, here was a niche that he could eventually fill. First he would have to find a suitable job and save enough money to train as a teacher. Then, as an educator, he could lobby the government for quality education for the farmers and their children. These grandiose dreams sustained him through hard times.

Bernard was rarely without his books clasped under his arm, tied round with their belt. This was his first escape from loneliness and poverty; more of his life was lived inside his books than in the cobbled streets of London.

As he left the East End heading West, he felt the weight lift from his shoulders. The streets grew wider. There were houses with patches of green in front. There were shops with displays that dazzled him. Trinkets, ribbon, frippery

- so much more than was needed for bare survival. He dreamed, as he neared his destination in Oxford Street, of a life not circumscribed by bare necessity. He enjoyed the feeling of books against his body. They allowed him to soar, in spirit and imagination as one day, he vowed, he would soar in life.

ANNA AND EDMOND

Eating in the home of his sister, Anna, and her husband, Edmond, a professor of languages, the adolescent enjoyed a foretaste of a life that was broader and freer. In London they had become his nearest relatives and it was a comforting feeling to have them close by now, and to see them so well established. They spoke perfect English. They dressed stylishly and, unlike many of the immigrant Jews, they interacted comfortably with Jews and Gentiles alike. Edmond spoke many languages and had tutored members of the Royal family. His school's letterhead read:

FRENKIEL' S SCHOOL OF LANGUAGES,
433, Oxford Street (halfway between Bond Street & Marble Arch)
London w.

Native Professors / Translations / Interpreting
English – French – German – Italian – Spanish – Russian, etc.

Though Bernard did not know at this moment where his destiny was to take him in his quest, he knew that one day he would be like them, possibly, in another country.

By 1912, Bernard had developed from a timorous immigrant in a new country into a socially self-confident young man. He lived in a flat annexed to one of the imposing private houses on Oakley Crescent, City Road, a very fashionable area in East Central London. He was comfortable with his peers and his elders. His English grammar was impeccable and he expressed himself eloquently in conversation. He had a flair for poetic writing. He had acquired bookkeeping skills and now had some business background. Overflowing with optimism, Bernard decided to emigrate to Canada.

BERNARD IN LONDON

Anna was not happy about his decision. She had become accustomed to being Bernard's "big sister" and adored having him in the same city. Since she and Edmond had no children of their own, in Bernard she had found an outlet for her motherly instincts. Bernard, being sensitive to her feelings, tried to break the news gently. He had been hinting about leaving London for some time, but Anna, not wishing to lose her brother to another country, had dismissed his comments as just chatter. First he told her that he was planning to leave London for "greener paths" and that he had considered a number of possibilities. Then he explained that for a variety of carefully considered reasons, he had narrowed down his choice. He had made up his mind to go either to Australia or Canada. Instead of arguing (as was her custom) she pleaded, "Please Sallie, Australia is too far away, we would never see you again. If you must go, at least go to Canada. Then at least there can be hope of you returning."

Anna and Edmond saw him off at Victoria Station. Anna's chatter was filled with advice and admonitions to her brother. From the mundane "Be careful you don't catch a chill on the boat. Wear your woollies," to the practical "When you arrive in Canada, don't be too shy to ring people. Ask for help if you need it." And of course, her frequent reminder, "Write us every bit of news as it occurs so we won't worry about you. Don't forget, you're still my baby brother."

On April 18th, 1912, four days after the sinking of the luxury liner the *SS Titanic*, Bernard, feeling invincible, boarded the *SS Sicilian* bound for Quebec, Canada. It was a typical foggy English day as he descended to steerage. He had heard stories of appalling conditions in steerage and had prepared himself for deafening noise, disgusting dirt, nasty odours, and intolerable crowding. Thus prepared, the bare accommodations on an enclosed lower deck did not surprise him. He had expected to be sandwiched in with more than a thousand other passengers in a tiny space. The air, he was warned, would be unbearably foul, reeking of sweaty bodies, tobacco, garlic, disinfectants, and the stench of the nearby toilets; the floor covered with vomit of seasick passengers. As it turned out, when news of the Titanic disaster had reached England, there had been a rush of last-minute cancellations, so the boat was only half full, contributing to more tolerable conditions.

The ship's food was coarse and crudely prepared and served on long trestle tables. The floor of the dining room was constructed of bare boards and was not kept clean. Moreover, all of the cooking smells from the adjoining kitchen collected there because of poor ventilation. But the sea passage itself was smooth and uneventful. Unlike some of the passengers who became seasick and could not look at food for days, Bernard was relatively unaffected. Blessed with a healthy appetite, he ate well, slept well, and most days were filled with excitement and anticipation.

The lower decks assigned for steerage passengers had no shelter, which meant that in inclement weather the passengers had to either stay down below or brave it on deck. With the reduced number of passengers, however, the upper decks were relatively spacious and accessible and Bernard got into the habit of walking about amongst the second-class passengers.

In second class on the same boat there was a young woman on her way to a teaching post in rural Saskatchewan. Her name was Winnie Hibbert, a stereotypical and prim English schoolteacher from a strict sex-segregated schooling background, with well-defined ideas of social behaviour. She wrote to her mother that she had been ill for three days and vowed she would never sail again (unless it was to return home to England). Her cabin, situated over the engine room, was tiny and poorly ventilated, and she "had to share it with three other girls." She also complained that it was difficult to sleep at night with the noise of the boat and the creaking sounds of the boards. She said she felt as though she were sleeping "in a basket."

She and Bernard met one afternoon on deck, and Miss Hibbert voiced her displeasure about the boat conditions to him. Properly sympathetic as was his nature, Bernard refrained from gloating about his ability to sleep anywhere anytime. He also refrained from describing the noises to which he was subjected, such as the horrendously vibrating engine, the banging of the hull against the waves, and the sliding of the steel cables.

He was vitally interested in her vocation. A teacher! That was the profession to which he aspired. She corroborated his belief that there was a demand for teachers out West and that jobs were plentiful. She was sharing her cabin with three other teachers - two elementary and one secondary - who were going to Regina, Vancouver and Toronto. In spite of the chilly weather, they passed a pleasant few hours, sharing ambitions and speculating about the Canadian West, about which they had both read so much.

One of the men in steerage class with Bernard gravitated toward him. They often took meals together, conversed, and compared backgrounds. Isaac, 40 years of age, had been born in Vilna, Russia, and like many married immigrants, was striking out on his own to prepare the way for his family to join him. The companionship was a welcome diversion for Bernard.

When the ship finally neared Newfoundland, the fog made the shore invisible. The ship's horn sounded every two or three minutes. Those Canadians who had crossed the Atlantic several times were not surprised. They said they had yet to see the place even from a few miles away. But the next day the fog cleared and land was sighted. Bernard was not impressed. At first sight Canada appeared to be a dreary place.

In the meantime passengers began changing their money to Canadian dollars. They received $5.80 to the pound. The schoolteachers wasted no time in inquiring about places to shop for clothes. Bernard found their chatter amusing. His mind was not on clothes at the moment, for he had no prospects of a job waiting for him with the accompanying salary. He had $99 Canadian in his pocket (a small fortune) and he was not about to part with any of it for frivolous reasons.

As the ship moved into the glorious St. Lawrence River near Quebec, Bernard could see the fir clad hills, the dales, the quaint streets with their many churches and pretty houses. The weather was grand and the scenery marvellous. He hungrily took in the mountains, hills and pine woods, little rivers, lovely islands, and lakes. The St. Lawrence was first narrow, then broad, then smothered in islands. The boat had to keep to a pathway in the river marked out by fir trees tied on to poles so that it looked like a road. Each time big rafts laden with pine logs passed by Bernard deeply inhaled their sweet fragrance.

CERTIFICATE OF SHIP'S SURGEON

I Hereby Certify that I have daily during the present passage made a general inspection of the passengers on board and that I have seen no passenger thereon who I have reason to believe is, or is likely to become, insane, epileptic or consumptive, or who is idiotic, feeble-minded or afflicted with a contagious, infectious or loathsome disease; or who is deaf, dumb or blind or otherwise physically defective or whose present appearance would lead me to believe that he or she might be debarred from entering Canada under the "Immigration Act" with the exception of the persons whose names are enumerated on the "Ship Surgeon's List for Medical Examining Officer" which I have prepared for such officer giving my medical opinion on the cases therein dealt with; and that there were no deaths or births during the passage except those mentioned on the said list.

The ship arrived in Quebec on May 1st, 1912, at 11:30 p.m. While the second-class passengers were exposed to cursory medical and civil examinations, the steerage passengers were scrutinized more closely. Bernard passed through the thorough medical inspection most satisfactorily, obviously young and in good health; the medical examiner was satisfied that he was not carrying any contagious disease. The civil examination turned out to be a different matter.

He was asked his age, his destination. Was he an anarchist? A polygamist? Had he ever been in prison? Who had paid his passage? Could he read and write? Did he have a job waiting for him? To the last question he replied that he did not have a job, but that he had experience as a watchmaker and that his intended employment in Canada would be in that trade. He displayed his letters of reference attesting to his character and work experience from his past employers, and also showed the impressive personal reference from Edmond Frenkiel, professor of languages. These documents, he hoped, would show evidence of his employability and usefulness to Canada. Unlike some of the other steerage passengers who were immigrants from Eastern Europe, Bernard was a British citizen, spoke perfect English, and needed no interpreter to translate his responses to the examiners.

M. Beaulieu, the civil examiner, took note of Bernard's references, but was not convinced he should pass inspection. The lad had no job, no relatives or sponsors waiting for him. After filling out the form with Bernard's responses, he stamped DETAINED beside his name, and sent Bernard to be further questioned by the immigration inspector.

Bernard held on tight to his papers. He had heard that many of the Jewish immigrants had been obliged to change their names when they arrived in Canada, but this would never happen to him. The Haltrecht name was sacred. It had been passed down for generations and it was his duty to carry it on.

Bernard found himself with two other men, both steerage passengers, the only three to be detained on a ship of close to 800 passengers. The other two men were also Jewish, and all three had listed their country of origin as Russia. Was there a connection? They had no way of knowing. One of the men was Isaac, the man who had befriended Bernard on the boat.

The immigration inspector looked over Bernard's form that had been passed over to him by the civil examiner. While it was true that the young man did not have a job waiting for him, he seemed employable, could read, write and speak English perfectly, and furthermore had a tidy sum of money to start off with. He did not appear to be a political threat to the country. To Bernard's relief, he was passed through.

A day later he and Isaac embarked by Canadian Pacific Railway on their trip to Montreal. Whereas Bernard knew no one in Canada, his new friend Isaac was acquainted with a family in Montreal, the Ratners, who had been his "landsmen" in the old country. Isaac's first stop the following evening was to visit this family. Would Bernard please come along? By the time the train reached Montreal, the two men's camaraderie had solidified.

When Bernard approached the house, his first impression was of candles flickering in the windows, familiar odours of Friday evening cooking, some girlish giggles, a father's remonstrations, and the warmth of a Jewish family home.

Here was a family of eight children, six girls and two boys, the same number as his own family. It was easy to see that the girls were the lively ones, especially the two little girls, Ida and Annie. Having been educated in Montreal schools, they wore the same assurance and confidence as Canadian-born girls.

Molly, the eldest, was plain, down-to-earth and practical. She worked in the family candy business. Next in age were Rachel and Rebecca, the two intellectuals of the family, although very different in outlook. Rachel was outspoken, an activist; Rebecca was a gentle and fragile romantic. Bernard's gaze turned to 16-year-old Dora.

Blonde and blue-eyed like her two younger sisters, she possessed an easy, unaffected manner. Slightly taller than the other girls, she had an oval face framed by waist-long, thick, wavy locks that shone under the soft light of the ceiling chandelier. Her delicate, peachy complexion was clear and unblemished. When she spoke, her voice was mellifluous and soft. To Bernard she projected the perfect image of a refined young lady unaware of her allure. During the meal she did not partake in the political discussion that ensued but livened up when topics of literature were raised. Since she and her older sisters often read the same novels, she could keep up with the discussion of authors, characters and story lines.

After dinner the family moved into the parlour. It was concert time. The children all studied music. They studied piano with Alfred Laliberté, the most prominent teacher of their time, and they studied singing with his wife, the former Lucienne Boucher. Isadore, the younger son, was learning to play the violin.

Luckily for the Ratners, this internationally recognized piano teacher with an extraordinary career had opened a studio on St. Denis Street in east-end Montreal. But before long, Laliberté had become disenchanted with the "thin-skinned" parents and their spoiled children who did not take kindly to his severity and his uncompromising attitude toward his students' work. And, because he was a non-practising Catholic, the local clergy campaigned against him. They told parents it was a sin to send their children to him. He abandoned his St. Denis studio to work on Saint Catherine Street West with the English and Jewish children whom he noticed were serious students.

The Ratner children were serious students. They all loved music and encouraged each other. On this particular night of Bernard's visit, Ida was the first to perform. Seated at the piano, she played a Chopin nocturne with sensitivity. Next, she accompanied the other family members in their various solos. Rebecca, the coloratura, sang "The Bell Song" from *Lakmé*. Isadore, too timid to offer a violin solo, played the obbligato with his sisters.

Bernard was enthralled by this unexpected soirée and when Dora rose to sing "My Hero" from *The Chocolate Soldier*, he was simply captivated. Not yet as accomplished as her older sister, Rebecca, Dora nevertheless had a sweet mezzo-soprano voice and her self-confident demeanor compensated for her lack of experience. Before long the whole family congregated around Ida at the piano for a sing-song of popular songs and light classical pieces. The Ratner family was used to having visitors, but they had to admit that this lanky young man stood out. "Tall, dark and handsome," as the girls later described him, with his expressive, reflective, intense brown eyes and shock of curly brown hair, he engaged each and every listener, discussing a variety of topics with a conviction tinged with diplomacy and tact. His presence was strong but natural. He listened patiently and intently to what each of them had to say.

He was also passionate about his ambitions. He told them that he was moving out West to obtain an education. He had a mission. He would train to be a teacher in order to educate the farmers in western Canada. Next he would influence governments to implement policies ensuring farmers' access to quality schools. The fact that he spoke eloquently (with a British accent no less), that he was extremely polite, and was also effusive in his praise of the family's hospitality, enhanced the overall impression of this young visitor.

When Bernard was leaving, he impetuously took Dora aside. "Miss Ratner," he began, "I would be much obliged if you would allow me to write to you." Seeing her look of surprise, he hastily added, "I hope you don't think I am being too presumptuous." Dora had been taken aback but only momentarily. She was deeply flattered to be selected for this honour. It made her feel grown-up. Without pausing to request her parents' permission, as she should have done, she willingly agreed to write to a perfect stranger.

2 ✿ DORA

On September 15, 1896, in the city of Vilna, a fourth daughter had been born to Samuel and Chvolas Ratner. They named her Deborah, later shortened to Dora, after the famous biblical prophetess and judge. The birth was a mixed blessing because Deborah's twin sister did not survive. The way the story was told to her, it had been a matter of survival of the fittest, and she, being the most persistent in her determination to enter the world, had pushed ahead of her sister. It was not her parents who discussed the graphic details of the birth. They kept silent about the event. Her eldest sister, Molly, claimed to have hidden under the table in their home to witness the happening, and she related her version of the story to Dora.

By 1900, 43-year-old Samuel and 30-year-old Chvolas were parents of six girls: Molly, Rachel, Rebecca, Dora, Ida, and Annie; and two boys: Max and Isadore. Thanks to their father's financial success as owner of the town's general store, the children were enrolled in the Russian Gymnasium. Attendance at such a school offered a superior high school education. Graduation from such a school meant possibilities of entry into some professions that were not barred to Jews, such as medicine, law or dentistry. Papa Ratner had ambitions for his children.

To augment his offspring's secular education, Samuel, a distinguished Talmudist and an authority on Jewish folklore, made sure that the children were well versed in Yiddish tradition and culture. He tutored them in these subjects and made certain they attended synagogue regularly.

Situated on the Wilja River, the city of Vilna, with its charming arches and cobblestone streets, was the centre of Yiddish life and culture in Russia. From the late 18th century to 1914 (Catherine II to Nicholas II) Vilna was under Russian rule. In this period the Jewish population expanded rapidly because of the May Laws of 1882 that prohibited Jews from living in rural areas. Forced to leave their villages, they moved to the large urban centres of Odessa, Kiev and Vilna. When Dora was a toddler, Vilna was considered to be not only the "Jerusalem of Lithuania" but also the cultural capital of Russian Jewry.

Samuel and Chvolas took pains to shield their children, especially the younger ones, from the Russian brutality that surrounded them. News of pograms carried out by the Czarist Russians were discussed by the parents in hushed tones. However, the older siblings, Molly, Rachel and Rebecca, could not help but be aware of the massive atrocities being perpetrated. Acts of terrorism were announced and discussed in the thousands of periodicals surfacing in the country. The girls read voraciously, talked of the situation with their fellow students, and debated the possibilities of taking action. Some students, still in their teens, were contemplating leaving their families to escape to safer countries such as England or America. Others were considering becoming activists in the revolution.

Descriptions of the horrendous Kishinev pogrom were still fresh in everyone's minds when two years later, in 1905, more than three hundred pogroms were carried out in cities throughout Russia. Dora was nine years old when Samuel and Chvolas began to talk seriously of emigration.

By 1908 discrimination against Jews throughout Eastern Europe had exploded into rage. Anti-Semitism had become so rampant that local anti-Semitic citizens were not only encouraged, but were officially sanctioned to rape and kill their Jewish neighbours. The Ratner family feared they would be next and decided they had no choice but to leave their homeland.

The two eldest sisters, Molly and Rachel, refused to go at first. They argued that they had to remain in Russia to complete their education. Rachel was studying dentistry and was planning to devote her life to this profession. Her other energies went into the right-wing Social Revolutionary movement which advocated destruction of the monarchy. She felt compelled to contribute to the ideals of a party which, come the revolution, would improve the lot of the ordinary people. She attended meetings, delivered pamphlets, and advocated the cause in spite of the risks.

It was these very risks that worried Samuel and Chvolas. However, they reluctantly agreed that it might serve their elder daughters better to complete their education in Russia. A compromise was reached and Molly and Rachel agreed to join the family at a later date. There were tearful good-byes but the family knew it would be a temporary separation. Only a year later, in 1909 when events became even more ominous, the two sisters also emigrated.

In the meantime, Samuel and Chvolas Ratner had arrived in Montreal with the other six children. Dora was 12 years old. Her youngest sister, Annie, was six. The Jewish population numbered close to 28,000, most of whom had arrived in the previous seven or eight years, also escaping from the tyranny of Eastern Europe. Some men who had been in Montreal longer were eking out a living as pedlars, but most men, women and children worked in the garment industry under substandard conditions. The recent arrivals were faced with a long, arduous road. But the Ratner family were not typical newcomers in several respects.

First, they arrived with some money that enabled them to start a small kosher candy jobbing business. Second, while most Jewish immigrants spoke little or no English or French, Dora and her younger siblings were familiar with both languages. They had studied English in Russia, and immediately after arriving in Montreal, they entered schools run by the Protestant School Board where French was included in the curriculum. When the older sisters, Rachel and Molly, arrived, private tutors were hired to enhance their English-language reading and writing skills. Within three months they were fluent in the language.

After residing for several years on Cadieux Street, a Jewish neighbourhood, it was time for the Ratner family to move on to a more assimilated environment. Samuel and Chvolas had built up their small business. They now owned a kosher candy factory that would subsequently include a retail store selling not only candy but a variety of items. Chvolas worked alongside her husband and they could now afford to hire a full-time cook.

The family had their sights set on St. Louis Square, a fashionable residential area that had been opened to the public 35 years earlier.

ST. LOUIS SQUARE

Its location, slightly removed from the downtown core, was most appealing to the Ratner family. Homes surrounded the green space with its picturesque cascading fountain in the centre, its shade trees, flowerbeds and delightful footpaths that would be a haven from the hustle and bustle of city life. Situated between St. Denis Street on the east and Laval Avenue on the west, it was familiar territory. A few blocks to the east and looking north and south was that great retail thoroughfare, St. Lawrence Boulevard, known as "The Main," a street predicted to be the "Fifth Avenue of Canada."

Finally they found a three-storey house for rent. Only well-to-do French Canadian families lived on this Square, including Mayor Louis Payette and an Alderman. Would a Russian Jewish immigrant family be welcome? Not to be intimidated, Dora took the initiative. Donning her hat and coat, she presented herself to the landlord, Monsieur St. Louis. She spoke to him in French. He agreed to rent the house to her family. When the family moved in, he was nonplussed to encounter a gentleman in European-style clothing and a long beard moving into his establishment. Although the man, Mr. Ratner, did not seem to belong to any of the ultra-orthodox religious sects (he didn't have the requisite sideburns, for example) he was obviously of the Jewish faith. Nevertheless, it was *un fait accompli*, and the family was ensconced amongst (or beside) their gentile neighbours.

Whereas Jewish immigrants tended to feel more secure living in predominantly Jewish areas, the Ratner family sought to live in more assimilated neighbourhoods. They thus became the first Jewish family to reside on 'The Square." They would mention this fact with great pride. Others may have lived "near the Square" but only their family lived "on the Square."

The St. Louis Square dwelling was spacious and easily accommodated Samuel, Chvolas and their eight children. Visitors were impressed with the interior of the house. There were three formal floors and a basement. On entering the vestibule, they saw an oak staircase that led to the second floor of the house, its bedrooms, and a huge bathroom. On the right there was an archway that served as the entrance to the wainscotted parlour, a sunny room with a piano. An oak mantelpiece was set above a welcoming fireplace. A double door with glazed glass panels led from the parlour to the dining room. An imposing crystal chandelier lit by gas lamps dominated the room and hung above a large dining table. The dining room led into a third room study.

All the rooms were ample, including the kitchen, which could accommodate the necessary tables and accoutrements required for such a large family. Many of the tops of the windows were trimmed with coloured glass panes in red, green and gold, adding to the aesthetic ambience of the home. As to be expected of superior buildings in this era and in this location, the ceilings in the room were high, measuring at least 14 feet. The dark oak floors nicely set off the oriental carpets.

The basement, with its finished rooms on the lower level, had been designed to be used for servants, and had its own separate outside entrance. It also had an interior staircase that led from their rooms to the kitchen. Since the basement extended to six feet above the ground and had its own windows, it felt more like a main floor. For a family of ten, every inch of space was welcome.

In some respects the family's day-to-day life was typical of Jewish immigrant life in Montreal, but in others, it was not. Like most immigrants, they had escaped from Eastern Europe with its discrimination and old world values and customs. They attended synagogue regularly where they mingled with other immigrants.

Most of the immigrants started out in factories like Wolman's, manufacturers of ladies' coats, the largest and best factory in town. Some trained as pressers, others as cutters, still others as lining makers. Many of them, both male and female, worked first as apprentices without pay in order to learn the trade, earning one dollar a week for six months, then five dollars a week. That type of work was not even considered for the Ratner parents or their grown-up children.

During the week the parents worked diligently at their candy shop. Most nights they stayed home and the children were required to be present for the evening meal. Samuel would preside over the table. Holding his glass of red wine, he would intone the Kiddush prayer in his beautiful tenor voice, then offer the benediction before slicing the bread. There would be much chatter and gossip about the day's events, after which those family members who had planned activities, such as outings to theatre, lectures or films, would depart for the evening. Except for Shabbat. Friday evenings everyone was expected to be at home. Following the evening meal, the many visitors invited for tea and cake would arrive. Saturday mornings they all went to synagogue and the day centred around the mid-day meal. Like many other Jewish families, the Sabbath was observed by such activities as walking, visiting and reading. One was not allowed to do anything that resembled work such as cooking, sewing, cutting or driving in any sort of vehicle, be it motorcar, streetcar or horse and cab. Samuel strictly enforced this Sabbath ritual. And of course, no writing was allowed, which meant no schoolwork for the children!

SAMUEL RATNER

Dora enjoyed school and was an above-average student. Her real enjoyment was English literature and she nurtured this interest by taking extension courses at McGill University in the evenings. Everything about the university thrilled her - the architectural ambience with its traditional stone buildings, the ample green space with its regal trees, the campus layout with its winding drive - and above all, the atmosphere of learning in the sacred halls and lecture rooms. She studied literature in particular and she wrote descriptions of the books she read in her letters to her friend Bernard.

She liked fiction mostly, reading Russian novelists such as Tolstoy and Dostoevsky, British writers such as Austen and Disraeli, and American writers such as Hawthorne and Garland. Poetry was her special passion and she would spend many an evening reading poems, first silently in her room, then aloud in the parlour to her family.

March 28, 1913

We are taking up Tennyson's poems and I like them very much. I am sure you must have read some of them, they are so sweet that when reading I feel like singing them. One of his poems is named "Dora." I think it is a very good one, perhaps I like it because it bears my name. I was so fond of it I learned it by heart and have recited it in our society.

Later on she would regret not having continued on to university full-time, but at the time it was more expedient to attend business college where she would take a course in stenography - short-hand dictation and typing. These skills would qualify her for a position; money was important to her because she wished to be financially independent.

30

Upon completing her stenography courses, she began looking in *The Montreal Star* classified advertisements. There was an opening for a stenographer at the Grand Trunk Railway. With her sisters' help, Dora prepared diligently for the interview. When the time approached, she dressed in her favourite sky-blue wool dress that matched her eyes, and went downtown. After interrogating her about her qualifications and giving her a brief typing and shorthand test, the Chief Clerk said, "We need someone immediately." "I can start tomorrow," was the quick reply. Pleased with the young woman's enthusiasm, the Chief Clerk said, "Excellent, then, Miss Ratner, I'll see you tomorrow. Nine o'clock sharp."

If the Ratners were proud to be the first Jewish family to live on the Square, Dora was also proud of the fact that she, a Jewish girl, had obtained a position with the Railway. Her parents, however, were concerned. Did the boss know she was Jewish? The topic had never been raised. "What about the Jewish holidays?" they asked Dora. "I'll speak to my boss when the time comes," Dora said.

As the High Holidays approached, however, Dora was not quite as cavalier. Perhaps her parents were right. She should have told the Chief Clerk at the first interview. But why should she have told him if he hadn't asked? She loved this job. What if he would not give her the time off? She would try to find the right time to ask, when the boss wasn't too harried with appointments and paper work - after lunch. People were always in a better mood after they had eaten, Dora had observed.

So after the mid-day meal, Dora cautiously approached the Chief Clerk. Mr. McCullen, a Scotsman, listened with some surprise. He had to confess to himself that he didn't actually know any Jewish people, although he had often seen immigrants on streetcars and walking in the east end of the city. But Dora didn't look anything like his conception of a Jew. With blonde hair and blue eyes, she was dressed similarly to any of the young women he knew - a Jewish girl who didn't look anything like a Jewish girl.

"Miss Ratner," he said, "I was not aware that you are of the Jewish faith. Please tell me about your holidays." Dora explained about Rosh Hashanah being the New Year and Yom Kippur being the Day of Atonement, and how important it was for her family to attend synagogue together on these special days. "Miss Ratner, you may certainly take the time off, and also for any other Jewish holidays your faith requires." Feeling very pleased with his tolerant attitude, he continued, "You just let me know in advance, so that I will be prepared for your absence."

That night, Dora, tickled pink, reported back to her family. "You see, you needn't have worried," she told her parents. Secretly, she sighed with relief. She was happy with the office environment where she had a pleasant working relationship with her co-workers. Also, she knew her boss was satisfied with her. And she loved the ambience of the district in which the office was located. Across from Grand Trunk headquarters was the impressive Albion Hotel, on the east side of McGill Street.

Commercial travellers or "drummers" as they were called, arrived at Windsor or Bonaventure Stations, then took the hotel bus or horse cab to the Albion. She could see them disembarking with their satchels and entering the lobby. Although she hadn't been in the bar of the hotel, her male co-workers told her that they sometimes drank whisky there for five cents a shot. They did not specify how many shots they imbibed at a time, but she suspected from innuendos that they often left the bar in very good spirits.

An agreeable job in a prestigious company, a large intact family in comfortable surroundings, a stimulating and pleasurable social and cultural life - these were the components of Dora's contented existence.

3 ✿ BERNARD IN SASKATCHEWAN, DORA IN QUEBEC

In contrast to Dora's idyllic home life, Bernard's life continued to be burdened with hardships. After his brief visit to Montreal, the highlight of which was meeting Dora and her family, he found himself in Cupar, Saskatchewan, a newly incorporated village with under 250 people, 40 miles northeast of Regina. What a culture shock after having lived in London and Berlin!

All the buildings were new or nearly new and built of lumber, the sidewalks were of planks and the streets were silty earth. Bernard soon discovered that in wet weather they became a quagmire. The main street, Stanley, was hub deep in mud every spring and the horse-drawn dray was often stuck. After the mud dried, a local farmer was hired to drag it out with his Hart-Parr tractor, which emitted a vile-smelling kerosene exhaust. Not all farmers had tractors, and teams of oxen were often seen in the village. There was no Social Aid in those days, but the Government supplied needy farmers with seed; the cost was charged as a lien against the land and repaid when a loan was taken out and a mortgage registered.

Bernard was interested in the farmers' access to education. He was told that Cupar School had started with a one-room frame house moved in from the country just southwest of the Village, and that in 1907 a two-room brick school was built. Each room had its own teacher. That was progress.

He decided to look for a job in a bank where he thought there would be more opportunity for advancement. There were two banks in Cupar, the Brass Bank and the Union Bank. Bernard opted for the Union Bank. Without too much trouble he secured a job as bookkeeper for the satisfactory salary of $40 a month. For his diligence and competence, in less than six months he was rewarded with a $10 increase. He quickly developed friends because people naturally responded to his warmth and earnestness.

Still, he needed to vent his disappointment at the primitive conditions in which he found himself to what he hoped might be a sympathetic ear. He picked up pen and ink and, in his first letter to Dora Ratner, described his journey and his impressions of Cupar. But first he offered a vivid description of the important day of his life when he had been fortunate enough to meet her and her family. In the most poetic language he could muster, he described the day, the hour, the weather, and his impression of every detail of the experience of meeting all of them. He didn't stop there. He painted a clear picture of each and every family member, leaving the impact of meeting Dora for the last. His letter reminded Dora of his manner of speaking when he visited her house. The eloquence of his written words reinforced that recollection. She told him that he possessed the gift of language. She wrote: "I cannot imagine that meeting me, one should write such words, that is, considering it as an event in one's history of life. It is beyond my comprehension indeed."

Although she had not said so, Bernard assumed correctly that Dora was keeping their correspondence a secret from her family. Their letters were posted through her office, partly because Dora had wanted to impress him with her office position. But she had not told her parents that she and Bernard were corresponding; she knew they would have thought it improper for her to carry on a correspondence with a man who was not only four years her senior, but whose relatives were across the ocean and unknown to them. Taken off guard, she had hastily acted independently. What harm could it do, to have a new friend?

When the morning mail was delivered to the office, Dora would quickly hide Bernard's letter in her top desk drawer. At lunch hour she would surreptitiously pull it out and tuck it into her purse to read on the streetcar en route home for the mid-day meal. During the meal with Rebecca, who also came home from her position at the Baron de Hirsh library, she would converse about other topics, deliciously keeping the correspondence to herself. Returning to the office, she would have an opportunity to look at the letter again.

Bernard was to discover, from her response to his complaints about Cupar, that 16-year-old Dora maintained a most positive attitude toward life. Bernard prided himself on maintaining his own positive attitude despite his history of hardships. He knew that, in Dora's case, her philosophy of life had not yet been put to the test. She lived a sheltered life in a cheerful family environment. She was also influenced by the literature of the time, which tended to be idealistic. He sensed that she was also positive by nature, even if this included a degree of naiveté that appealed to his protective instinct.

June 29, 1912
Grand Trunk Railway System

Dear Mr. Haltrecht:-

I have received your letter and am very glad to hear that you have reached Cupar safe and sound. I trust that you will be successful there and that your journey will be discontinued at last.

I can see by your letter that you have been met with good luck at the start, that is, have secured friendship, which people say, is a very rare thing to be found nowadays.

So you are complaining about the place being small, yes it is true, but very often people are better off in small villages living in a little cottage than if they were to live in big places. I will give an instance of a book that I have read lately and will try to make it as brief as possible, for I am very bad at telling stories, I prolong them too much.

Well, this book bore the name of *Hesper* by Hamlin Garland, it was published in 1904. Hesper is a lady of twenty and six, she was brought up in New York in a very rich home. Some years later she was forced to move out west to the Hesperian Mountains.

Her first impression out West was very disagreeable. She was used to meeting intelligent people, people of high rank and here, mind you, she only met cowboys. Besides that she was not at all poetically inclined to admire nature.

Well, she certainly changed her mind a little later. So you see, you cannot always tell....

Rather than allowing himself to feel imprisoned by the rustic conditions in which he found himself, Bernard made up his mind to acclimatize himself to the environment. His goal was not only to fit in, but also to become part of the community. Bernard met Mr. Gibbs, who was on the organizing committee for the annual community ball. When he invited Bernard to join him, Bernard readily accepted and threw himself into the project in his characteristic style. When the local paper described the dance as "one of the best ever held in Cupar," he and John were well satisfied with the results of their endeavours. Bernard's only regret was that Dora had not been present to accompany him.

To assuage his loneliness, days and evenings Bernard kept himself completely immersed in work and community activities, but it was at night that he keenly missed Dora. Lying on his back in bed with his arms crossed behind his head, he stared up at the bare ceiling in his room and imagined how sweet it would be to have her there with him, if only for a visit. In a rash moment he sent her an invitation to the ball, allowing himself to temporarily dream of her boarding a train, gazing out at the countryside, and finally arriving to his waiting arms, all the while knowing the unlikelihood of such a thing happening. When her letter came, he was disappointed but not surprised at her response.

December 2nd, 1912

Dear Mr. Haltrecht:-

I am sorry I had to decline your invitation because I found it a little too far a distance to go to a ball....

Some days later John Gibbs told Bernard that he was planning to spend Christmas with some relatives in Montreal. Bernard was enthusiastic and asked him to look up the Ratner family, and mentioned Dora in particular. When Mr. Gibbs arrived in Montreal, true to his promise, he telephoned, and as was their custom, the Ratners invited him to their home. This was Dora's chance to discreetly find out more about Bernard. She tried to inquire about possible rivals. When Mr. Gibbs was quick to point out that Bernard had made a number of friends, but did not have one particular close friend, she was satisfied.

Dec. 23, 1912

Dear Mr. Haltrecht:-

We have had regards from you by a gentleman who arrived here recently. He told us that you are working as bookkeeper at present. He has not stopped admiring you saying - you look a picture of health and beauty, and consequently you are the best man that he has ever met. This is very gratifying indeed.

As regards myself, I am well, working in the same place and am trying to make the best of everything. If you recollect, I belong to a society, that is, the "Young Women's Hebrew Association." Well, I am taking up Literature there. We have a very good teacher, she is a BA.

I am continuing my music lessons and my French lessons, so you see how busy I am. Please do not laugh at me, it is true, people say, if you will try to learn everything you will learn nothing, but I believe in Sarah Bernhardt, who advises learning a little bit of everything. I am trying to follow her example.

Dora's role model was Sarah Bernhardt (1844-1923), a famous French actress whose brilliant career commenced with the *Comedie Française*. Her flamboyant personality created controversy but her outstanding talent and charisma captivated audiences. When Dora spoke of emulating Sarah Bernhardt she was alluding to the numerous hobbies, adventures and activities in which Mme. Bernhardt reportedly engaged. She went up in flying balloons, rode live whales, was an accomplished sculptor, painter, and playwright, and had written a novel, *In the*

Clouds. Madame Sarah had even had a coffin made-to-measure for herself that she kept in her drawing room. She would lie in it from time to time in order to get used to it.

SARAH BERNHARDT

Montreal was on the itinerary of many renowned actors, and Dora and her sisters made sure to take advantage of the abundance of theatre offerings. A year earlier it had been announced that the Divine Sarah would be appearing at His Majesty's Theatre in Montreal. Although the actress was not young any more, they had never seen her perform, and this amazing opportunity was not to be missed. The sisters purchased tickets well in advance.

With handkerchiefs in tow, they readied themselves for the tear-jerking scenes they knew were in store for them. There was a hush in the audience as the star appeared on stage in the role of Soeur Beatrice in Maeterlinck's play of the same name. And the hush remained even at the close of each act when the spellbound audience dared not applaud. How could they interrupt the magic that had been created on the stage before their very eyes?

At the end of the play, Dora, Rebecca and Rachel rose to their feet with the other audience members. They applauded and applauded till their palms ached. There were ten curtain calls for Mme. Sarah Bernhardt. Even a hard-boiled critic like S. Morgan Powell of *The Montreal Star* unashamedly confessed that he wept openly while witnessing the heroine's death scene so marvellously portrayed by the inimitable Bernhardt. Not so generous was the critical review in *Le Nationaliste* the following day, which ridiculed the pre-publicity material that had underplayed the actress' advanced age. But the impression Bernhardt created that night would remain with Dora for the rest of her life.

Many was the night when she would close the door to her room to strut in front of the full-length gilded mirror, text in hand, imitating the divine Sarah's portrayal of Sister Beatrice. How wonderful it must be to be an actress! A star! To travel, to be applauded and adored by thousands of fans. To wear those beautiful costumes and to be made up. How magnificently glamourous! Even the mention of the actress in Dora's letter to Bernard would inspire her to rehearse later that night in front of her mirror.

Sarah Bernhardt may have been an indirect political influence on Dora. On her last visit, she had said that "women should clean out politics," albeit confining themselves to the municipal level. While Dora was proud of her reciting, singing and debating skills, she hesitated to mention her interest in the suffragette movement to the young men she knew. She preferred to avoid their unwelcome teasing and the defensive position in which the topic placed her, leaving that debate to Rachel, the activist. Rachel's influence was nevertheless close to home. She made sure to apprise Dora and Rebecca of every meeting, and strongly encouraged them to attend.

Bernard seemed different from the other young men Dora had met. She decided that she would test the waters by mentioning, *en passant*, in her next letter to Bernard, her interest in the suffragette movement. The sisters had not forgotten the cartoon that appeared in *The Montreal Star* in December 1912, showing a rotund, spectacled, middle-aged businessman reading the Sunday paper. His self-satisfied comfort is being disturbed by accounts of the militant suffragettes foolishly trying to disturb the natural order of things. The odious comparison

MILITANT SUFFRAGETTES
STILL MAKING FOOLS OF
THEMSELVES.

to the mosquito hovering above was an added insult. The sisters were still smarting from the ribbing they received from their brothers, Isadore and Max. (There has been another society formed here viz., 'Suffragettes.' They have very good speakers, so I drop in there sometimes....)

She need not have worried. Bernard, always open-minded, was democratic in his outlook. He believed in the ideals of equality. He not only supported the movement, he admired the women who were involved in the fight for their rights. Still fresh in his mind was their perseverance and heroism in London and their success, against what had seemed insurmountable obstacles, in gaining the vote.

Interested from an early age in political movements in general, he had followed newspaper accounts describing the promotion of universal suffrage for women both in Europe and the United States. He clearly remembered reading the word "suffragette" in 1906 when the word was coined in the London Daily Mail. Less than two years before, on March 19, 1911, while he was still in London, more than one million women in Switzerland, Austria, Denmark and Germany used International Women's Day to rally for the right to vote, to hold public office, and to attend vocational training. He was also aware of the celebrations that took place in Russia and China on that day.

Six days later, when he read that a fire at the Triangle Shirtwaist Factory in New York took the lives of more than 149 women - most of them Jewish and Italian immigrants - he was incensed. The suffragette movement, initially organized in New York to protect women in the factories who were being exploited, now had a tragedy to emphasize the exploitive and dangerous working conditions, particularly in the needle trade. The following year would see women rallying in Europe and America to protest the outbreak of the war, and to express solidarity with other women all over the globe. To discover that Dora, secure in an office position, and living a protected, sheltered life, was a supporter of the movement, only served to elevate Bernard's opinion of her. She was delighted with his response.

MAX RATNER

Dear Mr. Haltrecht:-

I beg to extend my thanks to you for being in favor of the suffrage movement, and also that your opinion of us is so high. I wish that every man would agree with you then the world would certainly have progressed.

Dora and her sisters knew that women in Canada, like their counterparts in other countries, had been struggling to gain voting privileges since the mid-18th century. What was taking place in the Prairies was encouraging. The prairie ladies, under the determined leadership of Nellie McClung, were launching an energetic campaign for women's rights.

Although Dora dropped into the Montreal meetings from time to time, she did not adopt a leadership role. Disliking confrontation, boisterous behaviour and fervent commitment to causes, she left political activism to Rachel. It did not suit her temperament and was not her style. Moreover, it offended her sense of propriety.

4 ✿ THE FATEFUL LETTER

Bernard had been visiting Regina, which he dubbed "a nice little city." While not London, England, by any means, Regina, with a population of over 30,000, was a welcome change from Cupar with its 250 inhabitants. Not that the city was completely out of the woods. Having been so recently self-sufficient, with an increasing population at the rate of one thousand settlers a month, a construction boom, and recognition as "The Capital and Wonder City" of its "mighty province," Regina was recovering from the sudden attack of a vicious tornado that wreaked havoc on this handsome city in June, 1912. Its restoration included the construction of impressive buildings such as the new Legislative Building, the new Sherwood Department Store and its first "skyscraper," the ten-storey McCallum and Hill Building.

Also prominent were the modernized civic services. Carrying revolvers, the police on the beat and their "mounted squads" on motorcycles contributed to the ambience of progress. The fire department no longer relied on volunteers. It boasted full-time salaried firemen who rode a shiny new red-and-white truck adorned with bell and electric horn and mechanized equipment. And the Regina rugby team retained its championship amidst the cheering celebration replete with a torch parade sporting flaming brooms.

Visiting celebrities such as Sophie Tucker and Buffalo Bill and his circus appeared in the splendid new Regina Theatre. Annual events, such as the Saskatchewan Music Festival and the local Fair, continued in an effort to entice people to settle in this city.

Added to these attractions, Bernard was interested to discover Regina's first synagogue. On Ottawa Street, the "House of Jacob" had opened that year with seating room for 400 ladies and gentlemen. Not that he was a synagogue goer. He had moved away from that ritual during his adolescent years in London, but it was nice to know it was there.

Wasting no time, Bernard had packed up his belongings and moved to Regina. In anticipation of the move, he wrote on December 11th, "On that day

[December 31st, 1913] at 1:30 p.m. I shall be on the road to the East from whence 'all wise men come'."

All was not wine and roses in Regina, however. The Canadian recession curtailed the city's business expansion and there was extensive unemployment. Nevertheless, Bernard remained optimistic. He would get settled, look around for prospects, and travel to Montreal for a visit. When a bookkeeping job in a bank was offered to him starting in the second week of March, the timing was perfect. He would put his goal of becoming a teacher on the back burner for the moment while he earned a living and tried to put some money aside.

When Dora received Bernard's most recent letter at her office, she tucked it into her top drawer as usual and continued on with her typing until her boss called her into his office to take dictation. She would wait to read the letter, wanting to savour every word. At the end of the day, she walked over to Dominion Square, found a vacant bench, shooed away a few brazen pigeons, and pulled the envelope with the familiar handwriting out of her purse. She settled down to read. She had been anxious to know how he was getting along in his new place.

Satisfied that he was adjusting well, she mused about how important the correspondence had become to her. Who would have thought this exchange would turn into such an exciting component of her life? And all in secret, too. Well, maybe one of these days she would confide in Rebecca. But not yet.

Dear Mr. Haltrecht:-
Your letter has afforded me much pleasure to hear that you are well and enjoying yourself. Joy makes people keep young and optimistic, joy is the soul of happiness, this in my mind is very good, as we will get old unwillingly.
I am sorry that your club closed so quickly.

Dora's clubs, on the other hand, had been thriving and were in full swing. One particular club was organizing a "Social Party" and each young lady was supposed to invite a gentleman. Although the Ratner home was always filled with "gentlemen callers" visiting the various sisters, and Dora was comfortable in their presence, the thought of being forward enough to invite one particular young man to escort her to a dance was somewhat intimidating. She professed to Bernard that she was more at home participating in the club debates. She was now preparing for her next debate on the topic, "Resolved that Reading is more beneficial than Travelling."

This Sunday our club is having a Social Party but the only trouble is, that it has been decided for each young lady to invite a gentleman, and especially when leap year is past, but I have never invited a gentleman yet, and being shy, I have not got the courage of marching up to one and asking him to come up with me. Is not this sad? I hope that you won't cry over it.

Dora's self-mocking humour was not lost on Bernard. It showed she did not take herself too seriously. He also thought (and hoped) it was her way of saying she missed him and wished he were in Montreal.

To counter his own loneliness, Bernard sought his own companions. He remembered that Isaac, whom he had met on the overseas voyage, had mentioned a Regina family by the name of Friedgut. He had asked Bernard to give regards from him if he ever landed in that city. Bernard wrote a short note of introduction, posted it to Mr. Friedgut, and was promptly invited to their home the following Sunday.

Isaac and Anna Friedgut had moved from the Ukraine to Canada in 1903. They came as farmers to a Jewish agricultural colony settled by the Jewish Colonization Association near Lipton, Saskatchewan. Like most East-European immigrants the Friedguts knew nothing about farming. However, they stayed five years on the farm before moving to Keliher, Saskatchewan in 1908 where Isaac opened a general store. In 1912 they moved to Regina and opened a furniture store.

Their home was situated on Victoria Avenue in the central part of the city. Unlike some of the poorer, more congested areas, the street had a tree-lined central divider that gave it a spacious feel. The neighbourhood was a mix of European cultures, with a predominance of German families. The Friedgut family had German neighbours on either side of their house. Since the Lutheran family on the one side did not speak to the Catholic family on the other side, the Jewish family of Friedguts had become a sort of intermediary.

When Bernard arrived at the Friedgut home he met the parents and their three boys and five girls. The parents were curious about Bernard's background. He was receptive, even eager, to respond to their questions about his roots, his journeys and his ambitions. The children listened with awe. Here was a person only a few years their senior who spoke from worldly experience.

As the afternoon wore on, the parents looked around their luncheon table and counted their blessings. Their family was intact. Here was a young man, separated from his family, struggling on his own. And yet he was filled with such energy, such optimism, such ambition. What an inspiration for their own brood, especially Abe, their eldest, who was only four years Bernard's junior. Upon his departure, they expressed the wish that Bernard would visit them frequently and consider their home his "home." Before long they invited him to live with them. They proposed that Bernard teach the children Hebrew in exchange for room and board and whatever he could afford. He gladly accepted their offer.

Bernard was thrilled with this family. The parents were unbelievably hospitable, and the children inquisitive and charming. It was, of course, to Abe, the closest to his own age, that he gravitated. Abe was evidently bright beyond his years.

After the visit, Bernard wended his way toward his rooming house in high spirits. At that time Winnie Hibbert, the young teacher he had met on his sea voyage, was living in Regina, and to add to his cheerful mood, they serendipitously met in front of a tea shop.

Bernard took the initiative and invited her for a cup of lemon tea. It was an opportunity to compare notes with someone else who was a relative newcomer to Canada from London. Winnie said she found Regina to be "an ideal little city." She enjoyed the fact that there was "no rowdiness and very little drunkenness or gambling." She said that her landlady, Miss Songhurst, had only heard of one robbery since she had come to Regina several years ago. Winnie herself had only seen about three policemen. That there was no workhouse as there had been in London proved her point, she thought. And she believed that good work and good wages were reasonably available.

Winnie had found a good listener in Bernard, who enjoyed her chatter. Next she moved to the topic of the cost of living, which she found high. The smallest coin was five cents and they both agreed you could buy nothing with it except stamps, newspapers and oranges. From her experience in church, she noticed that there were no pennies in the collection. To add to her dismay, marmalade was unknown, probably because fruit was so expensive, with the exception perhaps of apples and peaches. On the positive side, every house, no matter how small, was equipped with a telephone and electric lights.

In the district in which she lived, on 12th Avenue, almost every house was detached and quite different from its next-door neighbour and very often painted in different pretty colours. She said they were built in such quaint styles. Some had gardens in the front, some at the back and some at the side, so that they looked very irregular, she thought. But the rents were "extortionate."

All houses had mosquito net doors and window blinds. "The flies are in myriads," she exclaimed, but she was happy to report that she had not come across any mosquitoes yet, though some people she noticed were smothered in bites.

When Bernard inquired about the two teachers who had been her companions on the ship, she mentioned that one of them, Miss Benny, was also in Regina. And that whenever they happened to talk on the street, people, on hearing their British accent, turned around "so quick" to look at them. "It was not as if we raised our voices. We spoke very quietly," she assured Bernard. Had he had that experience, she wanted to know. Did people make comments about his British accent?

Bernard said he was not aware of people stopping and staring at him, but he had not been in Regina very long. He supposed he had become used to some comments when living in Cupar. He thought it was to be expected that people with whom he spoke would recognize that he was not Canadian-born.

"Canadians have a decided 'twang,' don't they, Mr. Haltrecht? I hope I don't get it," Winnie mused. How amusing, Bernard thought. He could picture the prim schoolteacher catching the accent in the air as though it were some kind of disease.

Having chatted for a couple of hours, they said their goodbyes, wished each other luck, and went their own ways.

Bernard was in high spirits. He was about to embark on a trip to the East, and a bookkeeping job awaited him in the West. The next evening, Monday, he boarded Train Number 8, the Trans-Canadian, and armed with lots of reading material, braced himself for the long train ride that would take him to the big city, to the Ratner family, and to Dora. He set his pocket watch for Eastern time. It was now 7:20 p.m. in Regina. In 54 hours and 20 minutes he would arrive at Windsor Station in Montreal.

In the meantime, he intermittently read and ate the sandwiches and fruit he had carefully wrapped. He snoozed, he gazed out the window at the incredibly blue prairie skies. He took in the wide expanse of snow-covered farmland through Manitoba and into Ontario, with its endless forest only occasionally interrupted by small villages, giving way, finally, to farmland once again, and at last the province of Quebec. From time to time he exchanged a few words with other passengers. Otherwise he contemplated his extended stay, during which time he would have the opportunity to spend more time with the Ratner family members and especially with Dora.

When he arrived, he was not disappointed. There was no shortage of activities planned. Bernard and Dora attended lectures, concerts, films, and theatre. On these outings they were always accompanied by one or more family members.

Dora immensely enjoyed Bernard's company. Had she not been anticipating this visit for the past year? However, she did not perceive the depth of his feelings for her. She did not realize that she had inadvertently won her correspondent's heart. Bernard was bursting to express his feelings, but he could not, since they were never given time alone together. So before leaving Montreal, he decided to profess his love on paper. But he was so anxious that she receive his message immediately that he forgot she had instructed him to send all letters to her office. He addressed it to her house.

Montreal, Que March 3rd, 1914

Miss D. Ratner
327 Cadieux St
City

My dear Miss Ratner:-

As we didn't have an opportunity during the last few weeks to exchange a few words privately, therefore, I trust, you will pardon me for writing you this letter on the day prior to my departure from this City.

Please always bear in mind that, whether you would not or could not have me as your chosen friend, I beg you, at any time under any circumstances whatever, whenever I can be of some service to you in one way or other, call upon me and I will always be ready to help you, no matter how much it might cost me; even if I have to pay for it with my own life. This is the only happiness I can hope for outside of you.

I wish you a life full of happiness and joy. May you never know of any sorrow or sadness; may everything you might do and anything you might undertake be crowned with success, and may your heart's desires, whatever they may be, find fulfilment in due time.

Farewell!! Farewell!! I will always remain,

Your sincerest friend

S. B. Haltrecht

P.S. Kindly accept the enclosed little book as a souvenir from me. Let it always remind you of him whose heart you have been the first one to win.

S.B.H.

As if this gallant, unreserved expression of emotion was not enough to emphasize his devotion, a day later, on his train ride home, Bernard composed and sent a boldly passionate poem for its time.

TRAIN THOUGHTS
dedicated to Miss D. Ratner

Dear, sweet, precious soul,
How hard it is to part.
I only just left Montreal,
And now we are apart.

When will we meet again?

Now be a good girl,
and write often to me.
What the German calls "guttenKerl,"
Is what I will try to be

Be happy and have good hopes,
For your future depends on that.
Let white "seraphin" robes
Always be your spiritual set.

Salek Bernard Haltrecht

This open expression of ardour came as a big surprise to teenaged Dora. A writing such as this changed things. Bernard was no longer a secret pen pal. This was a real declaration of love. It was thrilling and flattering but at the same time alarming. That night, she called her sisters into her bedroom to explain the situation. Molly and Rachel administered a mild scolding. Rebecca thought it

43

romantic, but did not dare say too much about it. The girls suppressed their giggles at the thought that Dora had the nerve to carry on this relationship in secret. The four of them put their heads together. It was unanimously agreed that the letter must be shown to their parents.

As expected, Dora's parents expressed their displeasure at their daughter's wilfulness. However, they did not dwell on it. She was properly contrite. After dinner, they held a family consultation. It was clear to everyone, Dora included, that she was not ready for this type of relationship. However, the family had become attached to this fine young man and did not wish to cut him off or to offend him in any way. Rachel came up with the solution. She, Rachel, would continue the correspondence in a cordial manner on behalf of Dora and the family.

Bernard, having poured out his heart to his beloved, anxiously awaited a response. Did Dora reciprocate his feelings? He could only hope she cared for him, at least a little. Waiting for the mail increased his impatience with the postal service. Surely she had written, where was the letter? Finally, one arrived. But it was from the wrong sister! Reading between the lines of Rachel's friendly but carefully worded letter, he understood the underlying message. The correspondence, and hence the relationship with Dora, was over.

Feeling acutely wretched, he was now forced to face the fact that he had been too hasty and presumptuous both in prose and in verse. He should have known better. But the way she had hung on to his every word, the way her eyes held his, had hinted at intimacy. Perhaps he had been wrong. Or perhaps she did care for him. Perhaps her parents were the ones who had insisted that she curtail the relationship. After all, she was young and they wanted to protect her from making any definitive plans prematurely. He had to face facts and look at it from their perspective. Who was he? Where was his family? Furthermore, he lived across the country, alone and without financial means. Naturally they would not consider him an appropriate suitor for their daughter - not now, at any rate.

Bernard was secure in the knowledge that he would prove himself. He would play by their rules; all of his letters would, from now on, be addressed to Rachel. It was time to initiate his educational plans. His desperate thirst for knowledge would lead him in the right path. In Regina while continuing to work as a bookkeeper, he would make inquiries about becoming a teacher. He would prove himself. There was no rush. Wait and see. Time would tell.

5 ✡ SCHOOLMASTER

The time had come for Bernard to initiate his plan to become a qualified teacher so that he could educate farmers' children. This had been his plan from the beginning, but especially because of the recent turn of events, he felt a sense of urgency to prove to Dora and her family that he was not just a dreamer but a high achiever. As luck would have it, a brand new Normal School (Teachers' College) had just opened in Regina.

Upon inquiry at the School, Bernard was informed by Mr. Blacklock, the efficient yet affable Registrar, that the entrance requirement for a third class certificate was the completion of Grade 10. "Once accepted," he said, "applicants receive ten weeks training. When grade twelve is completed, second class certificates become first class."

Mr. Blacklock felt it only fair to apprise Bernard of such a career's limitations. "Teaching commitments may be somewhat irregular," he said. "Because of impassable winter roads, some rural schools are open only during the summer months."

Bernard was not put off by this information. On the contrary, this situation would suit him perfectly. He could live on a farm and teach in the scenic rural areas during the beautiful summer months. During the winter he could reside and work in the city.

Fortunately for Bernard the need for teachers continued to be very high because of the thousands of settlers constantly pouring into the province. The influx of British teachers responding to the advertisements helped but the shortage still existed. In 1915, having completed the required training, Bernard earned his certificate from Regina Normal School. These teaching credentials would allow him not only to support himself at present, but also to support himself subsequently through university by teaching during the summers in one-room schoolhouses.

Bernard took to teaching naturally. Some of the students came from a variety of European countries, others were Canadian born. There were those who at first had a little difficulty getting used to his British accent. They snickered at some of his expressions. He took these responses in good humour, but made an effort to assimilate into the "Canadian" style of speech, or at least to acquire more "Canadian" expressions. However, he was very meticulous about teaching students proper grammar, as his years in London had persuaded him that good speech was the hallmark of an educated person.

The students, boys and girls, were all ages and sizes and at different stages of learning. It was a welcome challenge to keep them all occupied and interested. The girls all wore big bows of brightly coloured ribbon at the end of their plaits, or on top, if the plaits were bound round their heads. The mothers made their own and their children's clothes and taught needlework to their daughters while the boys learned farming skills.

The school building was surprisingly pleasant and the children mainly obedient. Bernard was a very patient teacher with those who wished to learn, as well as a demanding master with those who did not apply themselves seriously to their studies. Students in his classes were expected to exhibit courtesy, consideration and respect for others, as well as punctuality. If these attributes had not already been instilled by their families, they would be acquired in the schoolroom.

Attendance was the most difficult rule to enforce. Although there were 40 students on the books, it was rare for more than 30 of them to attend. Farming duties often kept them away until after the harvest when they all showed up for class.

The schoolroom was airy and spacious enough because regulations required 15 square feet of floor space and 180 cubic feet of air space for each pupil. It had to be well lit and ventilated, with a roomy porch for hats and wraps. Still, students need fresh air and exercise. So every day Bernard made sure that there were outdoor activities - skating and bobsledding in winter, playing ball and participating in track and field in summer. It was lucrative for Bernard. It paid $15 a week. Room and board cost $5 a week. Bernard could save a good amount of money.

Bernard was always planning several steps ahead. Yes, his occupation as a rural teacher felt rewarding for the moment, but he knew full well that it would not ultimately challenge his intellect. It did not assuage his hunger for a university education. Not having had the opportunity to complete high school, he could not be a candidate for university. So how could he gain entrance to University? By obtaining a BA he would simultaneously receive recognition from the Department of Education as "High School Master," specialist in certain subjects.

He knew what he had to do. He would start at the top communicating directly with the Premier of the province, Walter Scott. After all, Mr. Scott was also the Minister of Education. From his readings about him in the newspapers, Bernard gleaned that he was very warm and personable with a reputation for responding to letters from the public within a day of receipt. Surely that indicated care for his constituents.

So Bernard, a rural schoolmaster with no political clout, picked up the telephone and dialed the Premier's office. The secretary answered. Adopting a self-confident tone, he asked to speak to the Premier. "Whom shall I say is calling?" the secretary inquired. "Mr. Salek Bernard Haltrecht," he replied, adding, "I am an educator." "One moment, please," she said politely but officiously. Waiting nervously on the line, Bernard planned his little speech, not knowing at all whether he would have the opportunity to actually deliver it.

A moment later, to his extreme delight, the courteous Premier took the call and patiently listened to Bernard briefly outline his predicament. Scott, evidently surprised but equally impressed by the audacity of this young man, was intrigued. With a full schedule of appointments that week, he had to discontinue the conversation.

"Why don't you come round to my home, say Saturday next, at three o'clock, when we can chat more informally," Scott said. Bernard, astounded and thrilled, readily accepted. "I will be there on the dot," he replied.

This invitation was generous beyond his expectations. Arriving early, he waited outside the house so that he could ring the bell precisely at the appointed hour. Mr. Scott himself answered the door and warmly ushered Bernard into his study where a pot of tea awaited them on a silver tray. Bernard was taken aback when Mr. Scott said, "Please take a seat, Mr. Haltrecht. Now first, would you recount to me the story of your life?"

With such a distinguished captive audience, Bernard was in his glory. In his own quietly dramatic style, he narrated his story so far: his departure from home at an early age, his struggle for economic survival, his solo journeys from one country to another, his studies to become a teacher, and his now burning ambition to acquire a university education.

While Bernard talked, Mr. Scott appraised the young man. Meticulously dressed, obviously in his best three-piece brown suit for the occasion, replete with starched collar, a carefully chosen cravat, and large folded handkerchief peeking out of his breast pocket, he looked a picture of dignity and health. There was no clear indication of his Eastern European Jewish ancestry.

It was not often that Mr. Scott came in contact with a person of this background even though his party, the Liberals, depended on the immigrants for support. He could not remember any private encounters with immigrants of this ilk. It was clear to him that this was no ordinary young man. Mr. Scott viewed himself as a democratic and progressive leader. One of his other causes was the women's movement, and now he had an opportunity to help a worthy and deserving young immigrant.

"Leave it to me, Mr. Haltrecht," he told Bernard. I will see what I can do."

Mr. Scott was true to his word. His daughter, Dorothy, gave Bernard a list of the required textbooks so that he could embark on a program of study. Before long, he was deep into his books. While his counterparts were attending the local high schools, he was studying the same curriculum diligently on his own so that he could obtain his high school diploma and thereby become eligible to apply to university.

Bernard knew his timing was fortunate. Five years earlier, in 1912, the administration at Queen's University in Kingston, Ontario, had tried to implement measures to exclude Jewish students. But the outcry from the Jewish population across the country had compelled the Board of Directors to withdraw this part of their agenda.

There was another fortunate, albeit less prohibitive circumstance. Queen's University arranged that he sit for his examinations at the local rectory in Regina. When the day arrived, Bernard was nervous but confident. Even though he had studied the material diligently and absorbed it, one could never be sure of the questions that would be asked. Seated at the assigned desk, he waited for the signal to begin. At the signal, he picked up his pen and wrote non-stop, looking up only when the clergyman who was acting as invigilator called "time." Flushed with the adrenaline brought on by the experience, he handed in his paper.

Back at home Bernard anxiously awaited the examination results. He was on an emotional roller coaster. One moment he was euphoric, the next, despondent. One moment he was visualizing his life as a university student, the next despairing when no mail arrived. At last he received the envelope with Queen's letterhead in the top left corner. Hands shaking, he cautiously opened it, knowing his very future hung in that crucial missive.

Hurrah! His work had paid off. He had been accepted. Goodbye Regina, hello Kingston.

However, a small obstacle still stood in his way: his teaching commitments in Campbelltown, Saskatchewan. Fortunately Queen's had an extra-mural program to accommodate special students in similar situations. Students could keep up with their studies in the fall by correspondence and begin their residency in January. While schoolmaster Bernard, 24 years old, was still in rural Saskatchewan, his soon-to-be fellow students, most of them younger than he, were on their way to Kingston. By the time he arrived they would have established friendships and be immersed in their studies and extra-curricular activities. This knowledge did not dampen his spirits. He couldn't wait to join them and January was not far off.

6 ✿ COLLEGE BOY

On the train ride to Kingston Bernard was filled with anticipation. He had missed the shenanigans that went on with initiation but told himself he did not mind foregoing that frivolity. After all, at 24, he was so much more mature than those freshmen just out of high school. The exultation was more about entering the halls of higher learning.

At the station a student handed the few students a list of boarding houses. Then came the scramble for a room with an ambience pleasant enough in which to spend the term. Those arriving in January could not afford to be fussy. They would take what was available.

First on the list was a house at 83 Frontenac Street. He hurried over. The exterior, typically Victorian, with its red brick facing, bay window, and wooden porch, looked inviting enough. It reminded him more of London than of Regina. It was a two-storey plus basement and attic bedroom. Mrs. Selby, the landlady, greeted him pleasantly and showed him the last available room. It was spare, yet clean, with a worktable to serve as a desk. He counted himself lucky.

The next day classes began. His entry into the university, albeit sedate, was nevertheless thrilling. Finally, here he was, settled in, embarking on living the life of his dreams. He was a full-time university student, partaking in many aspects of college life. He thrived on his professors' knowledge; he made new, dynamic and compatible friends; and he was, most importantly, immersed in his studies.

It had now been almost three years since he and Dora had been in touch. Proud of his new status, he decided to take the initiative in an effort to resume

83 FRONTENAC

his correspondence with her. This time he would mind his P's and Q's.

Dora, looking over the family mail, saw an envelope with familiar handwriting addressed to her. It was from Queen's University. Her heart skipped a beat. Yes, he had written specifically to her. He wanted to revive their friendship. At last. The timing was right. Although she would never have admitted it, she had longed for a word from him since the abrupt termination of their correspondence. Now the situation had changed. She was a mature young woman of 20 and capable of handling her own affairs. Both of them wanting to restore their relationship, both of them not wanting to appear indiscreet, they coyly pretended that they did not know why their correspondence had been discontinued.

Montreal, Jan 21, 1917

Dear Mr. Haltrecht:-

I was rather surprised to receive your letter. I notice that you are blaming yourself for not writing to me for so long. I really do not know who is to blame. I believe I am partly the cause of it. As you are the one who broke the silence, I therefore take it for granted that we will let bygones be bygones and continue our correspondence.

Although I have not heard from you personally about your undertakings, my sister Rae told me of them and I wish to congratulate you and hope you will succeed.

As for myself, I am well, am still working in the same place and am trying as a whole to take life easy. I am taking up elocution, gymnasium and am also learning to skate. Some sport eh!

Please write and I will follow your example.

Your friend

Dora Ratner

Dora was pleased that she was learning to skate because she knew that skating was a relatively new sport for females. Tramping her way along the snow-filled streets with her skate laces tied together and draped across her shoulders, she felt emancipated, like a modern woman. Though her parents pointed out that in their generation no well-brought up lady indulged in such an unseemly activity, Dora could now benefit from the fact that the sport had been socially accepted.

Bernard enthusiastically responded to Dora's offer to continue the correspondence. And he let her know that he would be more reserved in his feelings from now on.

I wish once again to express my appreciation for your kind correspondence. I sincerely trust that you will continue this in future, and I thank you for it in advance. If I have in any way at any time, acted the way I should not, please forgive me. I look upon your friendship as one of my greatest blessings and I shall always try my utmost to prove myself worthy of my friend.

Impressed that Bernard had adopted the correct tone, and feeling secure in the propriety of the relationship, Dora felt free to be more bold in her own writing to him even on Saturday afternoon.

How many times had her devout father told her it was a sin to write on the Sabbath? But that was when she had some free time, so for once she would break the house rules. After all, she had attended synagogue with the others, so she had done her duty for the day. Still, she made sure she did not get caught so she would not have to endure her father's wrath.

January 28, 1917

Dear Mr. Haltrecht:-

Perhaps you are interested to know what I am reading now. It is a book entitled "Iliad" by Homer, translated by Pope. It is poetry and is so beautiful and full of music that I sometimes forget myself while reading it in the office and I begin to sing each line. I believe you must have read it, or rather studied it, as it is a work to be studied. Pope gives us a few lines expressed by Duke Buckingham:

> "Read Homer once,
> and you can read no more;
> for all books also appear
> so mean, so poor,
> Verse will seem prose;
> but still persist to read
> and Homer will be all
> the books you need."

I am taking a long time reading it. I am almost in love with some of the characters. For instance, Hector. How do you like my frankness?

On Friday night I went to moving pictures and saw "Friday, the 13th." I read the book by Thomas S. Lawson a couple of years ago. Frances Marion wrote the screenplay, and it was directed by Emile Chaupart. It is a picture of New York life, especially the Wall Street Stock Exchange. I enjoyed it very much.

Bernard, although most encouraged by her sudden openness, was not about to jeopardize the relationship a second time. He restricted his response to the literary aspect of her letter.

January 31, 1917

Dear Miss Ratner:-

You deserve to be complimented on the choice of literature. *The Iliad* is looked upon as the best of Homer's productions, and Homer is looked upon as the greatest of the ancient Greek classical poets. I know Pope is very enthusiastic about the ancient poets, Homer particularly, and advises all young writers follow their style. In his "Essay on Criticism," Pope says,

> "When first young Maro in his boundless mind
> work t'outlast immortal Rome designed
> Perhaps he seemed above the critics law
> And but from nature's fountains scorned to draw
> But, when t'examine every part he came,
> Nature and Homer were, he found, the same.
> Learn hence for ancient rules a just esteem;
> To copy nature is to copy them."

This is perhaps too great a praise for the ancient poets, nevertheless it is Pope's idea.

Now that the correspondence had been renewed and, for all intents and purposes, firmly established, Bernard was eager to share with Dora the experience of his travels and his accomplishments during the past three years. Whereas Dora's life and activities had remained stable, the past three years for him had been fraught with changes.

83 Frontenac St.
Kingston Ont.
Feb. 2, 1917

Dear Miss Ratner:-

Since I left Montreal nearly three years ago, I worked in more than one place and was engaged in more than one occupation. After going back west in the spring of 1914 I spent the remaining months of that year in Regina keeping books for one of the firms of that city.

During the 2 years of 1915-16, while the European nations have been manifesting their Christian Love to one another, I was far away from civilization in Northeastern Saskatchewan trying to impart a portion of my little knowledge to a few young Canadians. I had to fight too but my ammunition consisted of printed and written matter and not at all of the material used by other warriors.

I am enclosing you a copy of a song sung by the first year students at Queen's.

Freshmen's Song

We're the Freshmen of Queens College
and we always are in luck
For the less we have of knowledge, Boys,
The more we have of pluck.

Chorus:
Cacachelunkchelaly Cacachelunkchelaly,
Cacachelunkchelaly Cacachelunkchelaly (etc...)

There are many here before us,
And they are a jolly crew;
But they can't come Paddy over us,
For we're not so very few.
Chorus

We like the college customs well,
But cannot see the sport,
That he, who tries to court a girl,
Needs any other Court.
Chorus

Then here's to our professors, boys,
Of Anglo-Saxon Shute;
And those that make ideas sprout
From cube and classic root.
Chorus

And here's to each good pater
Who will rattle down the dimes;
And here's to Alma-Mater
And to good old college times.
Chorus

I feel very grateful to you for your kind letters to me, and I sincerely hope you will favor me with your kind correspondence continually. Your friendship is an inspiration to me in anything I do, and I shall try my best to deserve it.

Sincerely your friend
S. B. Haltrecht

7 ✿ QUEEN'S AND KHAKI

While Bernard was in his prime at university in Kingston, his sisters back in London, Anna and Irene, (Irene had moved there from Poland via Berlin) were missing him. Ostensibly worried about his welfare, over the previous year they had been using every bit of strategy to persuade him to return to England. They had reminded him that Queen's University was affiliated with all the leading British Universities, London included, so that Bernard could study in a city where he had relatives and friends instead of being in a place where "he knew nobody and nobody knew him."

On the surface, London was immersed in an atmosphere of joy with a fast pace largely created by the invasion of American culture. Slick and entertaining events such as American musical revues, ragtime, and silent movies enlivened the city. But underneath all this euphoria loomed a feeling of unease. His sisters were worried about his welfare, yet they were the ones living in a country in the shadow of war.

The shadow would soon become a harsh reality. In August 1914, war broke out all over Europe, and Great Britain declared war on Germany.

Almost overnight the atmosphere on the London streets altered. Uniforms - English and foreign - were seen everywhere. Women took over many jobs previously assigned to men. They conducted and drove buses and trams, they were porters and ticket collectors on railways and tube trains. Street lighting was painted dark blue. Hotels became government offices. There were shortages of food in the shops.

When in May 1916 the British Parliament passed a comprehensive bill for compulsory enlistment of all men between the ages of 18 and 41, the sisters' entreaties that Bernard return to England came to a full stop.

The British were not the only ones shaken by the Conscription Act. A number of students at Queen's expected to be "called to the colours." Most did not want to interrupt their education and risk their lives even for what was obviously a worthy cause.

As Bernard reported to Dora in his letter of February 11, 1917, "Many young men are worried, unsettled as to what they should do next. Let's hope the war will end soon, and life will again be pleasant and worth living."

Dora's life nevertheless continued to be "worth living" as she continued her classes at McGill and belonged to several cultural clubs, including the People's Forum and the English-language Book Club sponsored by the Baron de Hirsch Institute. Dora took pleasure in showing off its circulation library with its 3000 volumes to the newly-arrived immigrants and in introducing her sister, Rebecca, its librarian. Both sisters advised those not proficient in the language to enrol in its evening English classes. Dora's main interest was in the Book Club itself that provided a public platform for noteworthy speakers, local, national and international. Dora foresaw the day when Bernard would be an invited lecturer there. The People's Forum was a second club to which the sisters belonged.

March 4, 1917

Dear Mr. Haltrecht:-

Yesterday, being Sunday, I went to People's Forum and I heard a very interesting illustrated lecture by a Mr. Johnson, in town to deliver a few lectures on "Feeble-minded Persons." He has made a special study of them in India.

I have heard very little on this subject discussed before I may confess. He was so clear in his speech and rather humorous, although he had to deal with a sad story. It is, indeed, very pathetic to see some of those feeble-minded young men and women who look strong and vigorous (and some of them even possess good looks) to have to be so unfortunate.

He divided his talk into three parts: viz. the idiot, the imbecile and the moron, the latter name deriving from Greek "fool."

Like her contemporaries, Dora did not perceive the pejorative nature of the lecture. Instead she found the speech to be particularly enlightening because for many years in her walks around the neighbourhood, she had seen a young man sitting on his balcony making peculiar faces and mumbling incoherently. The lecture provided insight into his family's dilemma. She could more easily understand now why the family was taking care of their child at home. She admired them for it.

Bernard, meanwhile, was completely immersed in his studies and college life. However, he was not so cloistered that he was unaware of important world events. He and his fellow students had heated discussions about the war, the Czar, about capitalism and Marxism, about the bourgeoisie and the proletariat, and about the militant revolutionaries. Bernard, the only student born in Eastern Europe, was probably more emotionally involved in what was happening in Russia than the other students. Appalled by social injustice, he admired the revolutionaries even though it was against his nature - and his agenda - to be an activist. In March 1917, when Nicholas II, Czar of Russia, was forced to abdicate, Bernard empathized with many of his fellow Jews in Eastern Europe who were looking forward to a higher social, economic and cultural existence promised by the Bolsheviks. In a postscript to Dora he expressed the irony he found in the abdication. "P.S. From recent news it appears that even to be Czar of Russia is not a steady job nowadays."

Although Bernard wished he could spend the summer in Montreal, he was concerned he would not be able to find work there, while in the West he was completely confident that he would easily obtain a teaching position in one of the rural areas. Abe Friedgut, his Regina friend, was also planning to teach out West in the summer and his company would be a consolation. Dora, too, would have to be satisfied with learning of Bernard's news by correspondence.

May 18, 1917

Dear Mr. Haltrecht:-

I was delighted to hear of your success and wish to congratulate you most heartily. I was not surprised that you achieved 1st division, as I always knew you to be energetic and ambitious.

So now you are a teacher. Please teacher, write me how you find your pupils. Do you like them, and how are the surroundings in general out there? I am glad you have your friend, Mr. Friedgut, to keep you company..

Jasmin, Sask. May 21, 1917

Dear Miss Ratner,

You want "teacher" to tell you something about his pupils. All right! The "kids" are fine and dandy, not at all troublesome as one might expect. As long as they are all right the teacher is in good humour, otherwise there is something doin'.

The country around here is very nice: hills and valleys, rivers and lakes. I do a great deal of walking in the country every day. We have had nice weather already but the last few days were rather cold. Some of the seeded wheat has frozen and the farmers say that unless the weather changes immediately there is bound to be a bad crop this year which in addition to present existing conditions may mean actual famine.

Lovely pastoral surroundings notwithstanding, Bernard had some serious concerns. The newspapers were filled with the debate about conscription. On April 6th, the U.S. had declared war on Germany. On May 18th, President Wilson signed a conscription bill. Should Canada follow suit? What were the implications, not only for young Canadians as a group, but specifically for himself? It had taken him years of struggle to finally reach his present level of education. He was finally on the right path, teaching in the summer, studying the rest of the year at Queen's, a life he had dreamed of for many years. But underlying his success was the nagging worry of the unknown. At a moment's notice, he, along with his fellow students, could be recruited. An interruption in his studies now would bring additional hardship. Besides, fighting was anathema to him. It was against his nature.

The thing that now occupies the attention of most of the people in this country is probably the forthcoming Conscription Bill in the Ottawa Parliament. The newspapers try to make the easterners believe that the West is unanimous for conscription. Nothing is further from the truth.

The Western people - I mean of course the bulk of the people, the laborers - are just as much against conscription as the people in the East, only the Quebec people give a little more trouble to the authorities. Meetings are held everywhere opposing the compulsory scheme, and let us hope that Borden will at least once give ear to the demands of the majority.

Bernard realized that it was not an easy decision for Sir Robert Borden, the Prime Minister of Canada, torn between the opposition of "the bulk of the people" and the pressure put upon him by the Allies. A manpower crisis was calling urgently for reinforcements from Canada. Voluntary enlistments were moving at a slow pace. Returning from a special Imperial War conference in London, Borden announced in the House of Commons, on May 18th, 1917, his government's intention of taking steps toward compulsory recruitment. Although some young men were fired up with enthusiasm for the war, others, like Bernard, were deeply troubled.

The people of this district are mainly English and Scottish and whomever I talked to they are fiercely opposed to conscription, although the majority of single men of military age have enlisted voluntarily. I hope at least a ballot will be taken on this question, it is then certain to fail.

How are things in Montreal? We get some news of the uproars from the newspaper but I don't think we get all of it. Please excuse me for taking up so much space with the question of conscription. It is in everybody's mind, and it concerns everybody especially, of course, those of military age.

I wish you were here to keep me company for I feel lonesome, especially at night when I dream of having you here with me. Mr. Friedgut is nearby, but I meet him only week-ends; during the week we don't meet for we are several miles apart. Would it not be great to see you here? It would save writing letters, wouldn't it? Well, well, the end of May is here; then June, July, August, September.

If I am not forced to don khaki before the end of September, I shall stick to my plans and go to Kingston, which of course is not far from Montreal. "Thems" will be the days.

Happy dreams.

Your Bernard

June 15, 1917

Dear Mr. Haltrecht:-

We have rented a cottage in Strathmore, 30 minutes ride with the train, from Montreal, and I intend to be there every evening. It is a very nice place. The cottage is 5 minutes walking from the Station and is right near the river. Perhaps you can visit with us toward the end of August.

Jasmin, Sask.
July 12, 1917

Dear Miss Ratner:-

I trust you will not consider it rude of me not to have answered your letter before now. I have been feeling unwell of late and was even forced all last week to stay away from school. I was suffering from sore throat, but I feel much better now.

The doctor says I was walking too much in damp grass. Now what do you think I did in revenge? Just guess! —

I bought a little pony and instead of walking around the country, I shall be riding horseback. Won't that be lovely? Don't you envy me? If you come round to see me, I promise you faithfully to give you a ride on my pony, all right?

I am so much more fond of the country than of the city. Montreal would appear to me now a very noisy place, after spending the last few years chiefly in country places. It is strange how people can change. When I was in London I thought any place outside of London would appear to me dead. Now I have got so used to country life that I do not think I would care very much for city life.

Dora's earlier story about "Hesper" and the Hesperian mountains seemed to have proved a point after all. Delighted to have predicted this outcome, she read this letter aloud to her sisters. She also reminded Bernard of her earlier prediction, stopping short of actually saying, "I told you so."

Jasmin, Sask.
Aug. 13, 1917

Dear Miss Ratner:-

Although I cannot visit you in Strathmore, I promise I will visit you in the "mountain city" at the first opportunity.

Bernard envisioned romantic Sunday walks, picnics, and the view from the mountain lookout atop Mount Royal with Dora. He allowed himself to daydream to assuage his loneliness.

Dear Miss Ratner:

I am very anxious to see you as it seems an age since I saw you last. I sincerely hope you are all well and happy as I have known you to be. I sometimes feel a little miserable, at other times very jolly. You can feel sure that I shall feel in the best of spirits once I reach 33 St. Louis Square, Montreal.

In the meantime they were still following closely the news about conscription. Dora was glued to the newspapers when a serious clash between police and anti-conscriptionists ensued in Montreal after 500 young men attacked the *Gazette* building, smashing windows with bricks and stones. She reported the riot to Bernard, who had already read about it in the Kingston papers. But he had to carry on in his own rural world of educating youngsters, and his spirits were kept up by his enjoyment of the children, the countryside, and the extra-curricular fun that this environment offered.

Last Tuesday our school held its annual picnic. I was in charge of the races and games, etc. - and believe me I did my share of work. In the evening we had a dance in the schoolhouse and I enjoyed this part of the program better than anything else.

On Friday last, that is, three days after our picnic, a dance was put on in the neighbouring town where my friend Mr. Friedgut lives. What do you think we did? We went to it. Well, well, well! Two dances in one week. This is record-breaking for me. If I go on like this, you will expect me by the time I visit Montreal to be an expert dancer, won't you?

Sincerely yours, S. B. Haltrecht

Having completed the summer school term in Saskatchewan, Bernard was about to wend his way back to Kingston with a stopover in Regina to see the Friedguts. Then he would spend the next four days heading across the Canadian prairies. Normally Bernard would have made this trip through the United States but these days it was difficult to get across the border without tiresome interrogation and delays. He took the easy way out by travelling East through Canada. He was not a person to look for trouble.

8 ✿ SOPHOMORE

By the time Bernard returned to Queen's, the Federal government in Ottawa had decided that only Canadian citizens were subject to the draft. Since Bernard had not been "naturalized," and nor had Dora's brother Max, they were both ineligible. Her younger brother Issie was too young, as was Abe. As a bonus, Abe was now a freshman sharing living quarters with Bernard.

Bernard and his college mates, also too young to be drafted, all went out to the local pub to celebrate. They toasted the King, the country, the college and everyone and everything else they could think of. Bernard, free from worry over the draft, could now allow himself to enjoy some frivolities of college life before exams commenced. The freshman ball was coming up and promised to be a gala affair. He saw to it that his dance card was filled in advance.

> FRESHMEN'S RECEPTION
> CONVOCATION HALL
> QUEEN'S UNIVERSITY
> Friday Evng, Oct. 19th
> 1917

On the inside the names of the girls with whom he would be dancing that evening were listed.

After the excitement of the Freshman gala, it was back to college work. Bernard was cramming for exams. Fortunately, he had a photographic memory, and during exams, he was able to actually visualize the text book, turning the pages in his mind to "read" the text. In the midst of his studying, Bernard was also preparing for a debate about the Russian Revolution. Dora, supportive of his efforts, seized the opportunity to recount her experience of debating.

Oct 29, 1917

Dear Mr. Haltrecht:-

Our clock just struck nine. Perhaps the time when you are delivering your speech...The subject of your debate is a very interesting one and I hope you will win. I would certainly uphold the negative side, but even if you lose you should not be discouraged as it very often depends on the judges.

Judges are not always fair. I took part in a good many debates myself. I like debating very much. The last debate I took part in was "Resolved that censorship on fiction should be instituted in the State." I was on the negative, and the latter side won the debate. It was an interesting subject and discussed for the first time in Montreal. I don't mean to boast, but I was very much praised by the critic in my delivery. My opponent was a college girl.

POSTCARD

Nov. 12/1917

Just a few lines to tell you that I was pleased to hear you did so well in your debate. Thanks for the ribbon. I am wearing it on my new coat. Is that not an honor?

I went to visit Ida on Saturday at Macdonald College and had a very pleasant time. It is so interesting to see the buildings; you will have to visit it when you are here. It looks like a palace.

Wishing you success

Your friend, Dora

Dora was amused when Ida told her that Sir William Macdonald, the multi-millionaire benefactor of the College, was reputed to be so frugal when it came to spending money on himself, that he would often deny himself new clothing and even food items. For example, it was said that he would put either butter or jam on his bread, but never both at once. Too extravagant. The sisters giggled at the thought.

A week later, Dora, along with hundreds of thousands of citizens, rallied on a cold winter day to witness and cheer for what became a momentous event in Montreal history. A gigantic Victory Bond Parade with more than 10,000 participants was staged. Dora watched in awe as a long array of bands, floats, soldiers, and armoured cars headed by a tank promenaded from Victoria Square to Park Lafontaine via St. Antoine, Windsor, Dorchester, Mountain, and Sherbrooke Streets. And every inch of the way - on the streets, from windowsills, from rooftops - they were greeted by voluminous cheers from Montrealers of all ages and nationalities.

It was quite obvious to Dora and to everyone there that every detail was focused on one objective - the need to raise money to win the "Great War." The procession of floats depicting the various means to fight the battle underlined this need. The Canadian military, the soldiers, the navy men, the Red Cross, the Soldiers' Wives Leagues, the Daughters of the Empire, and every organization imaginable was represented.

She was especially thrilled to witness the newest ally, the United States, with its armoured cars, marching Marines, and its flag in full display, along with the British Marines marching and nodding modestly. She took in the French veterans, somewhat the worse for wear, participating proudly. She was surrounded by roaring ovations given by the fervent Scottish men sporting their bonnets and bagpipes. When the returning Canadian soldiers cheerily marched along smoking cigarettes, she noticed how much they were enjoying this relaxation of discipline.

The highlight, according to Dora, had been the chilling but thrilling rumbling by of the imperious tank. "Don't mess with us" was the clearly ominous message of the North American Allied Forces. The next day Dora would read *The Star's* description of it as "a thing without middle, beginning or end, a grim mediaeval monster that looked as if you could not get away from it even by climbing a tree, it was saluted with something like awe-stricken respect."

At the office she mulled over her attitude toward the war. Yes, she had been carried away by the patriotic spirit and the glitter of the parade. It was natural, she thought, that she should cheer for her own country. They had not started the war, they were bravely entering into it to support the Allies. She admired the courageous soldiers who were willing to give their lives for their country. But on a personal level, she did not want to see any of her friends or loved ones enter into such peril.

On December 6th, the war brought a tragedy of enormous proportions to Halifax harbour. The Belgian Relief vessel *Imo*, through human error and negligence, collided with the French munitions carrier *Mont Blanc* in the narrowest part of the harbour. The munitions ship blew a mile high in the world's greatest man-made explosion. Over two and a half kilometres of Halifax's industrial North end were totally levelled. The noise was so deafening that it was heard all the way to Prince Edward Island. Over 1600 people were killed and 9000 injured. Homes, offices, churches, factories, vessels, the railway station, and freight yards were all obliterated. A classmate of Bernard's whose family lived in the affected city was devastated to learn that his younger sister had been blinded by flying glass.

The Christmas break arrived and Bernard embarked on his long-anticipated trip to Montreal where the Ratner family would wine and dine him at their home. This time there was one markedly different aspect from the visit three years earlier when he and Dora were chaperoned everywhere they went. Now Dora was 22 years old and considered mature enough to have a special beau. On brisk sunny days they bundled up and walked arm-in-arm on the mountain or ice-skated on the rink. In dismal weather they went to a movie or to the theatre, or attended a lecture or concert. Dora proudly showed off her college beau at a Y dance and a social event, although his proficiency in the fox trot did not equal hers. Having reached this level of intimacy, Bernard now took the liberty of suggesting that they address each other by first name. She readily agreed to drop the formality.

When Bernard returned to Kingston and they resumed their correspondence, it was the first time in the six years they had known each other that he and Dora greeted each other by their first names. In early February, Bernard waxed poetic.

front - Rachel, Molly, Chvolas Ratner
middle - Anna Frenkiel, Ida, Annie Ratner
back - Dora, Bernard

February 8, 1918

Dear Dora,

Any time I take my pen to write you I feel possessed of a funny (or should I rather say strange) feeling which I cannot describe in words. I feel more like a poet than a prose writer, but as:

> Every poet as a rule
> Is deemed to be a fool,
> I shall certainly pose
> As a writer of prose.

Another school week has passed into the endless past never to return; one more week has gone into oblivion to return no more; and now I am spending Friday evening in its usual way. I am staying home: sitting in my cozy chair, I am trying to enjoy the spiritual company of absent friends. I meditate on the past, I consider the present, and I think of the future. The past is no more: sweet and bitter memories. The present will soon turn into the past: pleasant and unpleasant memories. But the future! Oh, the future! That is what we live for, and hope for. All the sweet and bitter memories of the past; all the pleasant and unpleasant occurrences of the present; must give way to her majesty The Future.

I can hear a voice exclaiming (with apologies to Wordsworth)

> Enough of poetry and art;
> Close up your barren verse;
> Come forth, and bring with you a heart
> That speaks plain English...

9 ✿ DREAMS

While the war in Europe was still raging, France and Britain officially announced their endorsement of Palestine as a Jewish State. A Zionist commission had been appointed to visit the Holy Land. On November 2, 1917, Britain pledged in the Balfour Declaration to actively support the establishment of a national home in Palestine for the Jewish people. As one would expect, this event had a deep impact on most Jewish people around the world and Bernard and Dora were not exceptions.

When Britain had earlier announced its willingness to hand over Palestine to the Jews, Bernard had been rather sceptical about the proposition, in fact, the turn of events seemed unbelievable to him even now. But this latest news from both France and Britain indicated that the Jewish future looked very promising. Incredibly, it seemed that the long dream of the Zionists was going to be realized.

February 17, 1918

Dear Dora:-

We certainly live in a great and wonderful age. There is more history created now in a week than there used to be in a century. I wish I could live in a great Jewish Centre where I would exchange words with leaders of Jewish thought and hear what they think of the latest developments.

Bernard's mind was occupied with historical trends, political theories, and current events. He admired great leaders who had come up the ranks from humble origins, like Trotzky, who had risen in less than a year from a struggling newspaper journalist in the slums of New York to become Minister of Foreign Affairs for Russia. He credited leaders such as Disraeli, Napoleon, and Bismarck with the possession of definite ideas, strong ideals and an iron will, all of which led them to achieve their goals. Whether or not he agreed with their goals was another matter.

As for political ideologies, what remained closer to his heart was his keen interest in the growth of Zionism and a Jewish state. What would his father have said had he been alive today? When he was a child in Poland they had discussed such dreams but never imagined they would be realized so soon. Although they had not been put into effect in his father's lifetime, amazingly, his son would be witness to such a great event. Many was the evening that Bernard and Abe discussed the topic.

Abe was a staunch Zionist, and he told Bernard he planned to prove it by enlisting in the Jewish Legion. He was forthright about his wish to see Palestine. Five hundred volunteers to the Jewish Legion were being recruited from Montreal, Toronto, Hamilton, Winnipeg, and points west. Together with U.S. volunteers, they were receiving military training at Windsor, Ontario and York Redoubt.

This was Abe's chance to prove his devotion to the cause. He was among those who signed up for duty with the armed forces to be stationed by the summer in Windsor. Bernard admired Abe for his courage, but like a devoted older brother, was also concerned for his safety.

Both students were hungry for news about the larger Jewish community in Montreal. With a Jewish population in Kingston of under 300, it was not surprising that there was little Jewish news. In Montreal, on the other hand, where Jewish people numbered close to 50,000, there was a bustling, active Jewish community.

Here in Kingston all the Jewish news I get is from the daily newspapers, which is very little. How are the Jews in Montreal now? Are they very active? Do they hold many meetings discussing the affairs of the day? I am very interested in the present day topics.

It is 12 o'clock midnight now. It is quiet in the room. You can hear the scribbling of a pen at the next desk where my mate [Abe] sits and writes an Essay on "Bismarck and the Making of Modern Germany." He is as quiet as a mouse and so am I. In the day time when we have a few moments to spare we always "chew the rag" over something or other: over Bismarck, Trotzky, Zionism, Socialism, Wilson, Marx, Napoleon, or over anything else, as long as we get something to quarrel about. Thus we live and spend the time.

Farewell, my dear. Happy dreams. Good luck.

Your Bernard

Dora, with her sister, Rachel, was attending some of the meetings and demonstrations that actively supported the Zionist cause.

Feb. 21, 1918

Dear Bernard:-

You asked me regarding the activities of the Jews in Montreal with respect to Zionism. They hold meetings quite frequently. There was a mass meeting for instance, a week ago, at the Monument National Theatre (arranged by the Poale Zionists) where the attendance was so large that hundreds of people had to be turned back.

Two speakers were brought from New York, namely, Dr. Zuckerman and Dr. Syrkins. The latter's birthday being that day, they presented him with flowers and a beautiful gift.

Dora admitted to Bernard that she did not attend this momentous political event. Having been invited to a sleigh ride, she let it take priority over a political rally. Her older sisters, Molly, Rebecca, and Rachel were going. It would be enough for her to hear about it from them and read about it in the paper the next day.

She did not regret her choice because she had a marvellous time, only returning home at 3:30 a.m.

I am going to the theatre tonight and I expect I will have a fine laugh, as it is a comedy entitled "Potash and Perlmutter" by Montague Glass. I saw them the last time they were in Montreal. This time the leads are being played by Jules Jordan and Charles Lipson.

The characters of Potash and Perlmutter, the bickering but good-natured manufacturers of suits and cloaks, were already known to audiences and their dialogue had become classic.

How Dora wished Bernard could share in these theatre experiences with her. She was longing to spend more time with him but she understood that for him to have a future, he had to complete his education, and studying had to be his priority. Eventually the outcome would benefit both of them. In the meantime, the Ratner household was being fitted with electric lights so it would have been inconvenient for him to visit.

The postponement was disappointing but rationally, at least, Dora knew it was for a good cause. The family had been looking forward to having electric lights installed in their home. The house still had gas chandeliers because their landlord, like many others, had been unwilling to invest too much money in his properties. In many cases landlords were able to get away with delaying renovations because there were always people resistant to change, who were satisfied to remain with their gas lighting.

Office 9:30 a.m.
Montreal, Que
March 13th, 1918

Dear Bernard:-

Friday evening I went to see a play entitled *Peter Ibbetson*, the author being Gerald Du Maurier. Originally, it was a novel. He wrote *Trilby* and a good many other plays. He had a wonderful imagination. This play is produced in the form of "fantasy." I believe it is the best play they had here for years.

There is a lot of dreaming throughout the play and the scenery is wonderful. The orchestra rendered the most romantic and enchanting music. It was so soothing that I was not sure that I was not dreaming myself Friday night.

March 16, 1918

Dear Dora:-

As you wrote me about Peter Ibbetson, I might as well tell you that I saw the play last Tuesday. It is the best show I have seen for a long time, although the plot has some flaws. The acting I thought was perfect: each actor on the stage acted splendidly. The scenery is grand, and the idea behind the play is very noble.

But the plot I think has many weak points: it is too sentimental and not true enough to reality. Besides I think a good deal could be cut out from the play without injuring the plot.

A good, perfect play should not have a single line more than is necessary for the plot. Take for instance the first act in the play: I think about half the characters could be thrown out without affecting the play as a whole.

Your Bernard

During the War there was a food shortage and several countries meted out ration coupons to their citizens.

March 14, 1918

Dear Bernard,

Here is a rhyme to amuse you.

"Our Sentiments"

My Tuesdays are meatless
My Wednesdays are wheatless
I am getting more eatless each day
My home it is heatless
My bed it is sheetless
They are sent to the YMCA.
The bar rooms are treatless
My coffee is sweetless
Each day I get poorer and wiser
My trousers are seatless
My stockings are feetless

My god, how I hate the Kaiser.

March 16, 1918

Dear Dora,

How comforting and how pleasant it is to receive a letter from you. I shall try to be cheerful all the time, for surely I cannot be otherwise when I think of you.

It was just after a class in Latin Literature, just after we had been discussing for an hour the literary style of Cicero, which in itself is enough to make one feel "blue" (excuse my slang) for the rest of his life, at 11 o'clock last Thursday morning. I went to the Old Arts Building where the students' Post Office is situated, and found your letter waiting for me. All I can tell you now is that I felt cheerful ever since. Thank you very, very much for your cheering words and encouraging statements.

 OLD ARTS BUILDING

It was taken for granted by students and faculty alike at Queen's that the female students were usually separate from the men. The men only could use the Student's Union. This arrangement did not change until after the Second World War.

Last night the Annual Arts Dinner of the University took place at the Randolph, the best hotel in town. It was what you might call a "classy affair." Five professors and over a hundred male Arts students were present, besides a number of representatives from the other faculties of the University. The dinner in itself was elaborate; college songs and yells were heard at short intervals. There was music in the air.

The programme consisted of toasts and speeches by the professors and the presidents of the different faculty organizations, and of musical numbers as well as readings and recitations. Everything was splendid and I think it was the best, the most interesting, and most pleasant affair that I have attended here since I came to Queen's. The short speeches were particularly good: informal, pleasant, humorous, pointed, and suggestive.

Here is Browning for you:

> The year's at the spring;
> And day's at the morn;
> Morning's at seven;
> The hill-side's dew-pearled;
> The lark's on the wing;
> The snail's on the thorn;
> God's in his heaven -
> All's right with the world!

Can you be as optimistic as Robert Browning? Tell me, I should like to know. Good luck, good fortune, happiness, joy, prosperity. May all these be yours.

Yours for ever.

Adieu!

Your Bernard

Dearest Dora:-

Now it is after supper, and I feel refreshed, sound and well, and ready for another night's work. My next examination (in Mental Philosophy) comes off next Monday morning at nine. Till then I am free. I shall surely be more than glad when I am through with the exams.

My last exam comes off next Friday, i.e. a week from to-day from 9 to 12. I expect that same night to leave for Montreal and reach your place Saturday morning. Grand and glorious won't that be?

In my last few letters I was constantly referring to the visit of Mr. Friedgut and myself to Montreal next month. Things, however, seem to be changing. Mr. and Mrs. Friedgut are urging their son to come home to Regina straight after the examinations; as parents they are anxious to see their child. Besides, poor boy, the thought that he is going to be home soon makes him feel the more home-sick, and he simply is wishing he could get home by aeroplane.

Of late he has been feeling very lonesome, and I did not know how to cheer him up. He has never before been away from home for any great length of time or for any great distance. Now he has been away for almost six months' straight, and for a distance of nearly two thousand miles so it is doubtful whether when the examinations are over, he will be able to keep himself from the first train going Westward.

He appreciates very much your kind friendship and thanks you very much for it. I, however, will be in Montreal in full force on Saturday morning April 13.

Gee, won't that be great to be in Montreal for the summer? Just think of it: St. Louis Square is the most attractive street in that city. Is it not? Aha!.

Goodbye for the present. Hurrah for next Saturday!

Yours forever

Bernard

10 ✿ ARMISTICE AND THE LAND OF BOOKS

Before Bernard's ecstatic departure to Montreal for the summer months, he and Abe spent an intense, nostalgic farewell evening together toasting the end of term and new beginnings. Having enlisted in Winnipeg in the Jewish Legion of Honour, Abe was on his way to serve with the Royal Fusiliers of the Imperial Army. This journey would take him both to Egypt and to Palestine until the fall of 1919. He then planned to return from the Holy Land to resume his studies at Queen's.

Bernard was naturally concerned for his younger "brother's" safety but at the same time thrilled that Abe was about to realize his long-time dream of seeing Palestine. There would be a stopover in London, England, and Bernard had sent a letter of introduction to Anna and Irene. Bernard was somewhat envious of this part of Abe's trip. He had not seen his sisters in such a long time.

He also would have liked to see Palestine, but not in khaki. He had his own agenda and his own romantic dream for the summer.

Bernard arrived in Montreal to a beautiful welcome from the Ratner family. The very next morning he walked over to Aberdeen School armed with his teaching and educational credentials and was hired on the spot. Thus began a glorious summer. Not only did he have a teaching position, but also Aberdeen School was just a stone's throw from the Ratner residence on St. Louis Square. He would get to see Dora every day of the week, and they could be in constant touch by telephone.

His only concern was Abe. He had not heard from him. He knew that Abe's parents had been upset and worried about their eldest son going off for such a length of time on what could be a dangerous mission. Bernard had been writing supportive letters to them, hoping to calm their fears and be of some comfort. In mid-summer, a long-awaited letter from Abe arrived, and Bernard was relieved to find Abe cheerful and full of optimism. He was about to leave for overseas and needed to share some intimate secrets with Bernard. As he said, "after all we are brothers, aren't we, old chap?"

NAVAL YMCA
#4715 Jewish Unit B.E.F.
Camp Fort Edward
Windsor, N. S.
July 26, 1918

My dearest Bernie,

I just wish I could see you once before I go overseas. I shouldn't like to leave Canada and the western world without seeing you.

I am enjoying camp life thoroughly. I have been promoted from the ranks and have it easy right along. Everybody is in fine spirits. We expect to go to England very soon, then we shall get a furlough and I shall go to see your sisters if at all possible. I intend to take O.T.C. in England and then go to Palestine to do what I started out to do.

I think I have won my parents over, and they are proud instead of sorrowful, father especially. You know how irritably built I was: how always dissatisfied. Well now I am enjoying peace of mind and a clear conscience. In a word I am at ease with the world, I love everything, am bright and cheerful. I like the fellows here - fine chaps - and they like me.

One boy, a young Manitoba City lad of 18 is my special companion and we are together always. We sleep in each other's arms and often (he's a very pretty fellow) we embrace each other in an honest-to-goodness, home-made kiss. He is in love with a little girl in Winnipeg and is as simple and loveable as a little girl himself. We find a kindred spirit in each other in more than one way (just a little confidence, Bernie, after all we are brothers, aren't we?)

I too am in love. She's seventeen, a graduate of Winnipeg H.S., a teacher, and one of the cleverest girls in Winnipeg. She's really the first Jewish girl I have ever met and so you can imagine my state of mind - nay my state of heart.

Let me quote a few lines from her letter. "If I could only be as you think I am, a Jewish Joan of Arc, if I could be at least, as Judith was (her own name is Judith) in the olden days I would feel as if I had some reason for existing. As it is, you don't know me at all, I am just a plain little Jewish girl who has to stay at home, while her heart is really in the struggle, and she's aching to shoulder a gun on behalf of her nation and her land, or do anything rather than stay at home."

Oh, well, I can't write any more now. Perhaps this will be the last letter I write to you in Canada. We are expected to leave early next week. My last word is "Would I could see you and have an old time chat."

A letter from Bernard's New York cousin who was in the American army in active duty did not share the optimism expressed by Abe. His letter was filled with disgust at "man's inhumanity to man." From the YMCA Camp Dix in New Jersey he wrote of being placed in the Field Artillery and of trying to get used to "this hard unhomelike life."

Meanwhile Bernard and Dora had been doing the circuit of picnics, dances, theatre, socials. There was no end to the round of activities they enjoyed together. And the family hospitality was beyond all expectations. On his departure to Queen's at the end of the summer, he felt so beholden to the Ratner family that he was too overwhelmed to adequately express his deep appreciation in writing. The precious time spent together during the summer months served to further intensify his relationship with Dora. She had openly become his "dearest."

Oct. 2, 1918 (10:30 p.m.)

Dearest Dora:-

If I could only put on paper all I wish to say to you, how happy I should feel. But alas! My power in the usage of the English language is by far too limited for me even to attempt to express all I should like to tell you.

When I look back on the summer that has just closed and think over the happenings in my personal career during the last five and a half months I consider this summer to have been the pleasantest in my life, at least the pleasantest of all my previous summers in this country. Just think of it! To be with you most of the time to see you every day, and to hear your voice every hour. It is more than I can scribble down with pen and ink. I hope you feel as I do, and I hope you as well as the rest in the house know how grateful I am for all the kindness shown me. I simply don't know how to thank you and I must drop it.

Yesterday, Tuesday morning, at half past nine I moved out of the G.T.R. station, Montreal, as you have seen. I was at once struck with the "blues" (pardon my slang) and began to feel miserable. The train moved through hills and valleys, through fields of grass and fields of hay, through prairie land and cultivated ground.

I sat quietly and observed it all from the window. I felt sad, melancholy, downhearted.

As soon as the train reached Cornwall I noticed some Queen's fans ready to join me. At Brockville more students entered the train, and by the time we reached Kingston we had enough fellows for a big picnic.

We talked a great deal as you can imagine. Some of the news was good and some bad. A few boys that graduated last spring are married, many are in the army, some of them in active service behind the firing line in France.

Now that the summer months with Dora were relegated to a memory, Bernard allowed his thoughts about other topics to surface. He contemplated the war, Zionism, and his own personal conflicts. It was one year after the November 1917 Revolution in Russia and civil war was still raging. The Bolsheviks had changed their name to the Communist Party and moved the capital of Russia from Petrograd to Moscow. These changes had occurred through terrorism and bloodshed and Bernard foresaw further massacres of innocent people, with no end in sight.

At the same time, the war in Europe was closer to home with young Canadian men having enlisted and gone overseas to risk their lives. Bernard admired courage and dedication to causes, but these were not the type of causes in which he saw his calling. His fighting would take the form of intellect rather than artillery. He dreamed of a day when he would be in a position to help people - Jews and Christians alike - survive in a better world. For the present, his immediate world was at Queen's. As a third-year student, he held the status of Senior. Some of the male students had enlisted in the army during the summer, others had transferred from Arts to Medicine, and new faces had shown up. The customary "Rush" decrees had been issued to the incoming freshmen and the Proclamations sent out.

Now that Bernard's relationship was on solid ground, he tried to play matchmaker with Ida, the pianist, and Abe. Notwithstanding the superlatives Abe had written about the girl called Judith, he knew young love was unpredictable and so just in case, Bernard could not help thinking, Wouldn't it be great if Abe and I could marry into the same family? Dora could be intermediary.

Tell Ida that Mr. Friedgut is very fond of music; classical, as well as popular songs; and although he does not play any instrument himself, he is a fairly good judge of music. He is a clever fellow, quick-witted, far-sighted, and a good judge on life in general. He is "young in years but in judgement old."

At the same time he dispatched a letter to Abe describing Ida as smart, pretty, a graduate of Macdonald College, showed talent as a pianist, and moreover, could bake wonderful cakes and make delicious candies. He sent his appreciation of Ida's efforts through Dora.

Also tell Ida that her candies are first class. The cake is splendid. The fruit came in handy on the road.

Good bye. Sweet dreams. Regards to everyone in the house.

Your Bernard

Abe had arrived in London, England, to a hospitable welcome. Anna and Irene were thrilled to cater to him and to pamper him and insisted he make frequent visits. During one of these visits Abe "spilled the beans" about Bernard's love life. Since Bernard had only hinted about his relationship with Dora, they were most intrigued. Abe also regaled them with the many stories about the Ratner family that he had heard from Bernard.

Irene immediately wrote Bernard gently chiding him for not having sent a photo of Dora. While she and Anna were charmed by Abe and happy to be in the company of their brother's dear friend, Irene wrote, "However pleased I am with him [Abe], I wish it were rather you instead, Sally, but not in his clothes." Not in his army clothes, indeed.

Meanwhile, the notorious Spanish influenza epidemic that had struck in the spring of 1918 in other parts of the world was occurring more frequently closer to home. At Queen's, faculty, staff and students were acutely affected.

The Ratner family was not exempt from this vicious epidemic. The two younger girls, Ida and Annie, were both ill. Dora, Rebecca, and Molly were devoting their energies to nursing their sisters. Dora was also worried about Bernard. But he was quick to assure her that even though the flu had struck Kingston, the city was not as seriously affected as Montreal, so far at any rate.

Oct 14, 1918.

Dear Dora:-

This goes further to prove that Kingston is not so bad off, otherwise they would not send their medical men out of town. However, this does not by any means mean that Kingston is free from the epidemic. No, many are affected. The hospitals are full of patients, and I know some students who took sick last week could not be taken to the hospital on account of lack of space.

The Selby family that I stayed with last year are affected: the girl Olive and her little brother have been sick for over a week while their mother walks around half sick. The house I am staying in now has escaped it so far and I hope will escape it right along.

The main thing is to keep cool. I hope that by the time this letter reaches you, both Ida and Annie will have fully recovered.

The Spanish influenza is not a dangerous disease by any means; all one has to do is to be careful: keep warm and get as much fresh air as possible.

This being Thanksgiving day we have no lectures. This gives me a chance to prepare a good, short essay on Hobbes, Locke, and Rousseau: their theories on "The Social Contract," which I have to hand in tomorrow at 10 o'clock. I like politics best

71

of all my classes (Prof. Skelton is the lecturer in this class on The Origin, Growth and Form of the State) including even History. I enjoy my studies, I like my room and am satisfied with my board. So you see, everything is well with me.

Thanks for the warnings you gave me about looking after myself. I am going to do as you say, but be sure you too practice what you preach. All right, dear?

Despite Bernard's admonitions to "keep cool," he himself had become afflicted with anxiety about Dora and her family. When Annie, the youngest, became critically ill and was hospitalized, Dora reluctantly accepted Bernard's offer to help. He rushed off to Montreal to pitch in, his appearance doing much to elevate the spirits of the family. On his return to Kingston he wrote:

Oct 30, 1918

Dearest Dora:-

Strange how time flies. It appears as if I had just - only a very short time ago - been in Montreal, now I am back in Kingston. Yes, I am back in my room; I am sitting at my table. In front of me are books of every description: histories, dictionaries, and text-books of all kinds. It was only yesterday that I was in the Canadian Metropolis and to-day I am in the Land of Books.

When Bernard had arrived in Kingston, he had gone straight to the College. The College grounds were quiet. He saw some students playing tennis and discovered that there was an enforced holiday because of the flu epidemic. All lectures had been cancelled. He was told that the College would re-open the next Monday, Nov. 4th. For Bernard this was welcome news as it would give him an opportunity to catch up on his assignments.

He went for a long walk, telephoned the boarding house to expect him for supper, and enjoyed the free time. After supper he had a long, interesting discussion with his English friend, a Christian Scientist, who invited him up to his room where he entertained Bernard with his violin. He played *Kol Nidre*, parts of *Bar Kochba*, and some Russian and Polish classical pieces - an unexpected treat.

The next morning Bernard received a package of letters from each member of the Friedguts in Regina. Bernard was happy to hear from them and with Abe so far away, he needed to maintain a connection with his Western family. By Sunday, November 3rd, almost all the students had returned and college was beginning to liven up. Within one week, on November 11th, the atmosphere livened up even more, not only at Queen's, Kingston, and Montreal, but in many other parts of the world as well. That was the day that World War I officially ended. On that day, Bernard, euphoric, dashed off to send a celebratory telegram to Dora's family.

7KF 10

KINGSTON ONT NOV 11TH -1918

MR O RATHER & FAMILY

33 ST LOUIS square MONTREAL QUE

CONGRATULATIONS PEACE, PEACE, PEACE LONG   LIVE DEMOCRACY HURRAH

HURRAH HURRAH .

930AM   BERNARD

At Queen's the celebration was exuberant. Bernard was awakened at 5:30 in the morning by noise in the street - whistling, shouting, yelling, and ringing of bells. He knew at once the war was over. He jumped out of bed, went into the next room, and dragged the two other fellows out of bed. They raced to 5 Princess Street (Main Street) and marched up to the College grounds. They entered Principal Taylor's house and ushered him out to deliver a speech.

They assembled at Convocation Hall where the Principal gave a short address announcing the cancellation of all classes for the day. He told the students to have a good time but to be careful so that he would not need to bail any of them out of jail. On the way from Convocation Hall Bernard was in the throng as they surrounded every professor they met and forced each and every one to deliver a speech.

During the day, parades of all kinds took place in town. The Queen's Students Grand Parade began at 6:30 in the evening at the College Campus and that entire evening the throng, stretching for two blocks, controlled the city. The students had their College banners out. Speeches were delivered in the Market Square before many thousands of people. They marched through the city and broke into every theatre and moving picture palace, but Bernard took pride in the fact that "not a cent's worth of damage was done."

Around 9:30 they all marched to the College gymnasium where an impromptu dance was held. The professors' wives served refreshments, and students and professors alike enjoyed themselves till one o'clock in the morning. For Bernard and his classmates, "that was the end of a perfect day."

Montreal had celebrated the war's end prematurely on November 7th, having heard rumours that it was over. By the noon hour, hordes of people had left their work to boisterously celebrate the momentous event.

November 15, 1918

Dearest Dora:

Your card of a week ago was a surprise to me and I did not know at the time what to make of it. I took it simply as a joke, but later I noticed in the newspapers that the people of Montreal as well as of some other cities thought that peace was here a week ago. But you see Kingston is more accurate. The Kingstonians did not celebrate till Monday.

The sobriety was evident two weeks later when the impact of the losses hit home. Six hundred thousand Canadians had fought in the Great War. Sixty thousand would never return. Queen's represented a microcosm of that loss.

December 3, 1918

On Sunday morning a solemn memorial service was held at the Convocation Hall in honour of the Queen's men who were killed in the late war. The service right through was very impressive. As the Principal read the names of the dead, all stood in respectful silence, and a thrill of admiration mingled with sorrow passed through the air. The list contained 148 names, but it is not complete yet. What a loss when you consider it is from one University only. The wounded and missing are many times that number. Thank goodness the carnage is over.

The war was over. Bernard and his fellow students who had remained at Queen's were proud of their male colleagues who had enlisted and equally proud of their female colleagues who had performed Sunday V.A.D. work in Queen's Military Hospital. They had entertained the soldiers, offering them compassion and company, and bringing them "goodies" on numerous evenings.

While the "heroes" who lost their lives in the war were acknowledged and mourned, there were 50,000 victims who had also lost their lives battling the deadly flu epidemic.

Bernard's salvation was his complete occupation with his social and academic activities, which had created diversions from the tragedies of the year. Since his interest and proven ability in oratory and public speaking and debating had been noticed by both his peers and his professors, he was once again chosen to represent his year in the annual inter-year debate.

Dec 3, 1918

It is the most important debate that I have ever been engaged in at College, for it carries with it the honour of the year.

The subject of the debate is: "Resolved that the farmers' movement toward amalgamation is as great a menace to the welfare of the Canadian people as are any of our trusts." The representatives of Arts '19 are on the affirmative, while we have taken the negative. The two men opposing us are final year fellows, fully matured men of wide experience, well informed, and splendid speakers. In fact they are considered two of the best debaters in the Arts faculty.

Thus we have hard opponents, but this fact makes it the more interesting. My colleague, however, is also a good, fluent speaker, and a well informed man. He is the English fellow of whom I told you a good deal about when I was last in Montreal.

Just think of it, Dora. All the pretty girls of Arts '20 are behind us and wish us every success. Their sweet smiles alone are a sufficient stimulus to make us do our very best.

The debate comes off at 8 o'clock Saturday evening in Convocation Hall before the Alma Mater Society of the University. Three professors are the Judges, and the student body the audience. I feel excited over it already, but I hope I'll be cool that evening as it is very important to be so.

Jan 12, 1919

The night of the debate came. At eight o'clock my colleague called on me, and we both went to the Convocation Hall to meet our fate. I tried my best, and our worthy opponents did their best. It was an exciting evening. The judges retired after the debate and in three quarters of an hour returned to give their decision. Everybody in the hall became quiet. We all listened attentively to the criticism. The judges thought it was a good debate, a close one too. But nevertheless they unanimously decided that the negative (i.e. our side) won it.

Hurrah for arts '20! Congratulations! Good luck! Ha! Ha! Ha! etc. etc.

These were the shouts heard when the decision was given. Our worthy opponents immediately came up to us, shook hands with us, and congratulated us. Then a flow of hands from all over. There was enthusiasm, life, excitement, right along.

After the meeting adjourned about twenty fellows went down town to the restaurant and we had a big feed. The President of the Arts Society was with us, so he acted as chairman. After the supper everyone in turn was called up to say a few words. Then we had a few college songs and quietly dispersed. I got home about 12 o'clock.

I am very glad the whole blooming thing is over. I was so glad over the results that I could not fall asleep for a few hours after I went to bed last night. It certainly gives one pleasure and satisfaction to know that he "has got it," although I am at any time ready to admit that our opponents put up a good fight and did remarkably well.

Last night we had our annual Conversazione and we certainly had a splendid time. Dancing till 1:30 in the morning.

College is livening up; there is more life in it now than there was this time a year ago. This is no doubt due to the end of the war, therefore, we can expect great times next year. McGill and Toronto have had their Colleges closed for too long a period on account of the flu, and so they are on the rocks now. But Queen's has steered ahead of them all and is having its social functions as usual, in fact more than usual. There is music in the air.

And so the new year, 1919, struck a positive and successful note following the tragedies of war and illness of the preceding year.

11 ✿ DAYS OF JUDGMENT

After the armistice a new set of problems arose for Canada. With 100,000 men returning home from the war, unemployment became a serious issue. There was an onset of labour disputes and strikes, particularly in the munitions plants, which during the war had worked at top speed. Rising costs of food, gas and rent contributed to the general discontent. In contrast, at Queen's the mood and spirit of the college were considerably elevated. Enrolment, which had declined during the war years, was now higher and Queens' halls were filled once more. There was a feeling of great optimism about future expansion, and college festivities thrived.

One day, as Bernard was walking across campus, a student he had never seen before approached him and introduced himself as a native Kingstonian. He told Bernard that he and some friends had organized a Jewish Young Peoples' Club and were inviting him to become a member. Their purpose was to establish a Zionist organization. Meetings were held on Sundays, which could fit into his schedule, and the student also offered to introduce him to some local Jewish people. Bernard was definitely interested, even excited. However, the first meeting took him by surprise.

February 3, 1919

Dear Dora:-

When I got there I discovered that my name was on the program as the principal speaker of the evening.

What do you think of such a shock?

Though he was comfortable in the gentile ambience of Queen's, Bernard was nevertheless always pleased to meet other Jewish people. Since there were only about 50 Jewish families in Kingston, and he spent most of his time on campus, he did not normally come into contact with Jewish families in the town. Many of them were merchants whose small businesses were located on Lower Princess Street, which local residents referred to as "Little Jerusalem."

Members of the Jewish community were only too eager to seek out Jewish students to include in their house parties. In a small Jewish community there was always the worry that their daughters, having limited choice of young Jewish men, might fall in love with a "goy" and, God forbid, wish to marry outside their faith. Bright Jewish ambitious lads attending university were ideal prospects.

When the Levinsons, a Jewish family, invited Bernard to a party in honour of their son recently discharged from the American navy, he enjoyed the evening even more than he had expected. The absurdity of a mock wedding, replete with a *chupa* [canopy] and enacted by two young fellows, portraying bride and groom, and a mock Rabbi delivering the sermon, had everyone in stitches. A welcome relief from the seriousness of study.

A student night at the theatre was also scheduled and Bernard was looking forward to it because it had been a while since any shows that he considered worthwhile had been performed in Kingston. Shows in the town were largely limited to the Grand Theatre although some live theatre was performed on Queen's campus at the Grand Hall and Convocation Hall. In Montreal Dora had her pick of a great number of "legitimate" theatres and Bernard took pleasure in imagining her at the theatre and enjoyed reading her descriptions of the plays she saw. It was a way of sharing their mutual experiences. Their discussions about stage plays and films continued to be a major part of their correspondence.

Hearts of the World was an episodic saga revolving around a French family separated after the outbreak of the War. *Intolerance,* by the same director and also starring Lillian Gish, was a mammoth project shot on a massive, majestic Babylonian set which sprawled over more than 250 acres of Hollywood. It had an enormous cast of 50 actors. However, Bernard, seeing it for the second time, was disappointed.

Feb 11, 1919

Dear Dorochka:-

Your description of "The Wanderer" is splendid. I now feel sorry I did not go to see the play when it was in Kingston. There is great charm in imagining the pure, simple, carefree life of primitive people. Both scenery and acting are attractive, and the naive mode of living is interesting to study.

Since I returned from Montreal after the Christmas Holidays I have only been to two shows. First I saw "Hearts of the World." One has to acknowledge that it is a great, magnificent piece of undertaking by the talented director/writer David Wark Griffith, with a large cast of outstanding actors, [Noel Coward, Lillian and Dorothy Gish] but its ideas did not appeal to me. It is emotional propaganda commissioned by the British government.

The other show I attended last Wednesday was "Intolerance" and I was disappointed in it, after seeing it two years ago. In the first place there was no music (by the way there is a strike of musicians going on in Kingston) and you know without an orchestra a film loses a great part of its value. Particularly in "Intolerance," the music being chiefly oriental, adds so much to the charm of the picture.

Secondly, all the noise of the towers falling was entirely absent. When I saw it two years ago, the noise was almost deafening, now there was no noise at all. Again the picture itself was changed somewhat. Some of it was omitted. In a word it was not half as good as when I saw it for the first time. But in spite of these deficiencies, I am still convinced it is the greatest production that has ever been shown on film.

February 23, 1919

Dear Dora:-

I wish the next two months move up quickly and then I shall be - where? I shall be through on April 22nd at 5 p.m. That means I'll be in Montreal on the morning of April 23. It will be grand, won't it?

Movies and theatre aside, the couple enjoyed physical activity. Their principal sport was skating. Bernard skated every day and he called it the "best, pleasantest, and healthiest of all sports." Not being particularly athletic, the non-competitiveness of the sport appealed to him. He also loved being outdoors in the cold winter weather. Knowing that Dora preferred warmer weather, he was thrilled that she had kept up her skating. Bundled up, braving the cold, she, together with her sisters, would walk over to Parc Lafontaine, where they were sure to meet many of their friends.

When Bernard was not skating on the frozen lake, he would go over to the university's insulated primitive hut constructed of corrugated steel. Although it was referred to as an indoor rink, the interior was no warmer. The little stove it housed was totally inadequate for the size of the rink and could serve only to warm one's hands at a close distance. This hut was where Bernard's more athletic classmates, Abe among them, (who had returned from military duty safe and sound), practised hockey. Although Bernard was not on any of the sports teams at Queen's, he liked skating on their ice and enjoyed watching Varsity games.

For the moment he did not know that Dora had received unexpected news. The Grand Trunk Railway was having major financial problems and was on the verge of declaring bankruptcy. This presented a dilemma for Dora, who had worked for this company since graduating from business college. The impending bankruptcy was due to a number of reasons, such as construction costs, absentee management and expansion. Several serious accidents had also contributed to its demise. When one of the trains collided with and killed Jumbo, the famous circus elephant, world-wide attention was centred upon the scene near St. Thomas, Ontario. There was talk of the federal government taking over the railway. Now the company was forced to lay off many of its employees. There was much speculation among the office staff. Who would stay and who would be asked to leave?

Dora was luckier than most other employees. She was asked to continue on a part-time basis. Just as she was deciding how to respond, she learned that the Canadian Jewish Congress was being established with its headquarters in Montreal.

For several years Canadian Jewry of different sects (orthodox, conservative and reform) and of different socio-political ideologies (Labour Zionists, left-wing socialists, and Jewish nationalists) had been struggling to come together to form one united organization. But meetings always ended in controversy and acrimony.

The Montreal Jews were at odds with one another. They found themselves divided into the Uptown (Westmount) Jews and the Downtown Jews. Each group had a totally different idea, for example, of charitable causes. The Downtowners, mainly immigrants from Eastern Europe, were fervent about sending money to the European Jews who had been displaced during the war, whereas the Uptown, more assimilated Jews, were interested in raising money for Montreal charitable institutions. The issue had come to a head in 1915 when of the $24,000 raised in donations, the powerful Uptowners took it upon themselves to donate $1,000 to Palestine, $6,000 to the War Victims Committee, and $17,000 to Montreal charities. The Downtowners felt betrayed and angry.

The Ratner family had heated discussions on the matter. In some ways they were caught in the middle. They were not uptown Westmount Jews, many of whom were second generation Canadians. Yet they, and particularly the younger generation, were assimilated into the Montreal English-speaking Jewish community and were all involved in Montreal charities. The parents were torn between reminding their children of the plight of the Europeans from which they were fortunate enough to have escaped, and sheltering their loved ones from the horrors of war. They took obvious pride in their assimilated, accomplished offspring. They had immigrated to Canada to provide them with not only freedom from physical harm in a safe country, but also the educational and social advantages they would enjoy in a free society.

In the previous years leaders of the divergent groups had organized national meetings in different parts of the country. These meetings were an attempt to unite into a national congress with the aim of lobbying for a national homeland and declaring rights for Jews worldwide, but all attempts ended in dispute and failure. Shortly after the war ended, an American Jewish Congress was formed, and Canadian Jewry was inspired to try again. Under the leadership of H. M. Caiserman and Lyon Cohen, the latter representing the wealthy Westmount Jews, a democratically elected Congress was formed.

Queen's University
Kingston, Ontario

March 19, 1919

Dear Dora:-

It must have been quite exciting as well as interesting to be able to exercise the franchise and cast a vote. Did you not feel yourself very important? Before the elections everybody is nice to you, trying to get your vote. Such is politics...

The excitement directly affected Dora because the Canadian Jewish Congress was hiring temporary staff. Her sisters were urging her to apply for a job there. She was hesitant because of her attachment to the Grand Trunk in particular and because she was not fond of change in general. However, she reluctantly took their advice and applied for a secretarial position. Her application was accepted and she was offered a job in the head office. The timing was propitious. Not wanting to worry Bernard when he had exams on his mind, she had been making light of her work situation. Now that she had obtained this new position, she let him in on the good news without telling him how she felt about leaving the ambience of the Grand Trunk.

Hearing the news of her new position, Bernard congratulated her and encouraged her to consider continuing at Congress permanently. Perhaps in doing so, he was projecting his own ambition to serve the community.

But Dora was not convinced. She had her own preferences. The more reserved gentile ambience of the Grand Trunk was more appealing. Besides, over the years she had made friends in that office. A consolation was that they had agreed to keep in touch.

Bernard, typical of university students, complained of the interminable "plugging" for his final exams, but true to his fashion, he nevertheless managed to find the silver lining.

A week from next Monday (April 7) examinations begin. Thus the days of judgement draw nigh, when you are forbidden to smile heartily, when you are prevented from enjoying life, when you are in constant dread of what is coming next.

But still this is the beauty of life. If not for dark and dreary days, we could not appreciate bright and cheerful ones; if not for suffering and sorrow, we could not enjoy happiness and joy. Only a hopeless pessimist finds no bright spot in this world, but I hope we do not belong to this dreary class of people.

In case you find this letter incoherent, please do not blame me entirely for it. While I am writing this, there is music in the air downstairs. The young lady is playing some charming tunes on the piano, and therefore I find it rather difficult to concentrate my mind on anything.

She is just now playing the song, "Till We Meet Again," [composed by Raymond Egan and Richard Whiting] and I think it is a very charming piece. Don't you think so? I am very often carried away by the music into some higher world, and feel tempted to go downstairs to the parlour to sit down and listen to it. But it is too late in the term now, and I simply have to do without that pleasure. I hope, however, to get good music in Montreal during the summer.

How is Ida? Tell her I'll like her ever so much if she practices up some of the latest pieces of music, including the one mentioned above...

It would surely be nice, if I had been able to be in Montreal for Passover. However, I may be at a Seder this year, something I have not witnessed for a very long time. I have been invited to a Jewish family's home for the first Seder evening.

Are you going to steal the Afikomen? Better confess, and tell the truth.

Well, good luck, good fortune, happiness, and prosperity to all of you.

Your Bernard

Like all Jewish families, every year the Ratners celebrated Passover, the Festival of Freedom. They adhered strictly to each part of the ritual, from changing every dish in the house to discarding every bit of food that was not kosher for Passover. *Matzoh* (unleavened bread) replaced bread for the full eight days. During the hurried departure of the Israelites from Egypt, they did not have time to add yeast or to knead their mixture of bread dough. The dough, carried on their backs, baked without rising in the hot desert sun. In the Seder ritual, part of the Matzoh is the Afikomen, which is hidden for the children to find later and be rewarded with a gift. Since the Ratner Seder did not involve children, Bernard amused himself by teasing his adult girlfriend about "stealing" the Afikomen.

At last the school year was over, and Bernard, euphoric, packed up his bags. He was off to a summer teaching job in Montreal where once again he would be close to Dora, where they could see each other every evening and weekend, where they could talk intimately, where he could declare his love in private, and could see with his own eyes that she returned his devotion.

Dora's natural diffidence in expressing her feelings was very obvious in her letter writing. When they were together, however, she let go some of the reserve and he was reassured of her deep affection for him. It was becoming a long courtship but it would be worth it in the long run when Bernard had a position, was able to financially support a wife, and they could be together in the same city. Whenever he raised the topic of the years of separation still ahead, Dora reassured him that she was in no hurry to marry, that her life was full, she could wait. Instead, she said, he should concentrate on his studies and not worry about her state of mind, she was happy.

Dora was happy on two counts. Not only did she have her beloved with her for the entire summer, but also a few of her friends from the Grand Trunk had crossed over to work at the Canadian Pacific Railway, and had persuaded her to follow suit. So she was now working in an office at Windsor Station, the terminus of the Canadian Pacific Railway. It became the paradigm for a distinctive style known as the Canadian Railroad Chateau Style. Dora planned to continue to be

DORA & COLLEAGUES General Publicity Rm 318

employed by the C.P.R. until her marriage. And now, with Bernard near her, life could not be rosier. An added cause for the family to celebrate was Annie's graduation from Macdonald College. She had followed in her sister Ida's footsteps, Ida having graduated two years earlier.

After a delightful summer, Bernard returned to Queen's to find the city abuzz with excitement and expectation. Prince Edward, Prince of Wales, heir to the throne of England, planned to visit Kingston. The university hosted him as befitted a royal guest. The newspapers reported that "Wherever he went, His Royal Highness won friends and devoted admirers by the charm of his smile, his unaffected modesty, and his unspoiled youthfulness."

One admirer he did not win over was Bernard, who did not find him to be at all charismatic.

ANNIE AND IDA RATNER Middle Row

October 29, 1919

Dear Dora,

Last Saturday the Prince visited Kingston and Queen's, which honored him by making him an L.L.D. graduate of the College. So in the near future I hope to be a fellow graduate of the same university as the Prince of Wales. Some class!

When he entered the hall at Queen's, he walked up the platform holding both his hands either at his tie fixing it, or straightening his collar with his fingers. He appears to be a shy, young, nervous boy.

I think you could make a better princess than a prince. Besides, you are a princess, anyhow. You are a princess to me. Is not that sufficient?

Well, look after yourself, sweetheart, and don't worry. The world is yours, and you are going to be happy all your life.

Yours,

Bernard

It was Thanksgiving weekend and Bernard and Abe were visiting the Ratner family. Bernard was in his glory, showing off both his "princess" and her warm, hospitable family to his best friend. A big fuss was made over the two students who were spoiled with food, excellent music and lively conversation. Evenings Ida sat at the piano, and the others gathered round to sing.

The two lovers were given time alone to spend together while Abe was looked after by the sisters. Abe was full of praise and he constantly complimented Bernard on his splendid taste. As the romance had intensified, the parting produced even more than the usual melancholy.

Nov 10, 1919

Dearest Dora:-

When I think of yesterday this time I feel possessed of a mixed feeling of both gladness and sorrow. Gladness, because I think of the sweet moments I was spending in your company, and sorrow because those moments are moments of the past.

I need hardly tell you of the happy week-end I had occasion to spend in Montreal and which terminated at eleven o'clock last night. The week-end passed like a pleasant dream. But no, it was not a dream, it was a reality. Your dear presence made the week-end for me the most enjoyable one I have had for quite a while.

When the train pulled out of the Grand Trunk Station, the two of us sat down, facing each other, but uttering no sounds. We opened one of the satchels, took out the apples, each taking one. Abe soon fell asleep, and slept till the conductor announced that we were only two miles from Kingston Junction.

I sat all alone thinking and meditating the greater part, and slept only for about half an hour. We reached Kingston City at nearly four o'clock in the morning, and went to bed at half past four o'clock. At seven o'clock I was up again and at eight I was at the lecture room discussing James Stuart Mill's essay on Liberty.

Thus the night passed. It was a miserable night, considering the pleasant evening I spent the night before. I felt like singing

Tell me why nights are lonesome;
Tell me why nights are blue
Tell me why all the sunshine comes
Just one time when I'm with you.

Why do I hate to go, dear
And hate to say goodbye?
Now somehow it's always so, dear,
And if you know, dear,
Please tell me why

This song was just appropriate for the occasion, and believe me if I had heard music, I would have sung to it with all my heart and soul. I sang it in my heart anyway. You can tell Ida I have enjoyed her music more than ever. Good bye dear sweetheart. I hope time may pass quickly and I may be able to see you in the near future once again. Be good, dear child.

Your Bernard

Aside from his studies there were many distractions to ease Bernard's loneliness. He sometimes led discussions at the local Y, entered essays into various contests, and wrote letters to the editor of *The Montreal Star*. One topic was "The Jews and Bolshevism." In his letter of November 19th, he told Dora:

I just want people to look at a question from every angle, and not from one side only. Many people have the habit of either praising the Jews and raising them above the seventh sky, or constantly finding fault with them and dipping them down to the lowest gates of Hades. We are no more and no less than other people. We have our faults with others, and we also have our good points. It's no use being narrow minded. We land in no place.

Bernard was intrigued with Bolshevist principles. To him a society in which the proletariat would be on equal footing with those in privileged positions seemed utopian. He could never forget the contrast between poverty and wealth during his adolescent years in London. And it certainly seemed that the Bolsheviks, unlike revolutionaries in other countries, were trying their best to adhere to the ideals presented during their uprising.

LOOK AT BOTH SIDES
The Editor, Montreal Daily Star

Sir: In a recent issue of your paper appeared a letter signed R. E. Hutchison, resenting the unfair attitude taken by John Alexander towards the Jews in their relation to Bolshevism. Mr. Hutchison treats the subject in a fair, but rather inadequate manner. While it may be true that a number of Bolshevik leaders are Jews, it should not be overlooked that a great many anti-Bolshevik leaders, too, belong to the Jewish race. On account of their abnormal existence as a people, the Jews naturally have produced types of mind that are extreme in their views - but extreme in both ways.

Trotsky, the Bolshevik (a Jew), refused to participate in the Berne Conference because he considers it not radical enough: Gompergs, head of the American Federation of labor (another Jew), refused to take part in the same conference because he considered it too radical; Marx, founder of the modern scientific socialism and fierce anti-imperialist, was a Jew; Disraeli, one of the greatest of British imperialists, was a Jew, too. Thus it runs right along. Therefore, for the sake of justice and fair play, let us look at both sides of the case. In Russia at present many thousands of Jews are confined in prisons because they are anti-Bolshevik in their leanings.

I hardly think it was Mr. Alexander's willful intention to misrepresent the Jews as a people, It is no doubt lack of information that caused him to make such erroneous remarks about a race, who from time immemorial, by sacrifice in blood and treasure, paved the way for universal liberty and brotherhood.

Kingston. S. B. Haltrecht

Bernard felt privileged to belong to the Political Science Club at Queen's because its membership was restricted to honour students in Political Science, History, and Philosophy, with the professors of these departments as honorary members. Meetings took place on a rotational basis at the professors' houses.

Bernard was particularly interested in the topic of discussion at the previous meeting, "What can we learn from the Bolshevist Regime as regards our own institutions?"

I was the first Speaker. After me came a sturdy little Scotsman taking post-graduate work in Political Science. Then the general discussion opened and questions were fired at me and at the second speaker both left and right. Three professors were present and they made short speeches at the end.

The general opinion at the meeting seemed to be that while we should not care to have a Bolshevist Regime in this country, nevertheless the Russians should be given a chance to experiment in any form of government they wish. I think this is a quite fair and sensible view.

The meeting took place at the home of Professor Skelton, and I had the pleasure of meeting Mrs. Skelton. She is a very pleasant woman. We were served tea and cake and home-made candy at the end of the discussion which lasted from 7:30 p.m. to 11:30 p.m.

In contrast to the intellectual level maintained at the Political Science Club, a vivid description of a "wild" students' night at the theatre followed.

Dec 6, 1919 (2:45 p.m.)

Dear Dora:-

In the "Gods" the yelling, shouting, and noise was something tremendous. Whistles, horns, College, Faculty and Year yells were thundering throughout the building. A number of pigeons were brought in and they were flying all over the place.

In the first balcony the lady students were sitting, while downstairs, professors and their wives and families as well as students that were fussing filled the place. From the Gods the students threw down peas, beans, confetti, rolls of paper, powder, and whatnot. In every way it was a wild night.

The play that was staged by the students was "Trelawny of the Wells," a comedy by Arthur W. Pinero. There is not much of a plot. I only wished you could have been present to witness the affair.

In the evening the results of the elections will be out and then there will be some further excitement. The main thing I am interested in is that the students should try and get reduced rates on the railways during the Christmas Holidays, and that we should not have to pay full fare. Don't you think this is important?

Well, what shall I say further? My body is in Kingston, but my heart is somewhere else. I am thinking about two weeks from now. Can you imagine such pleasant thoughts? Hurrah!

Well, be good dear child.

Yours Bernard

12 ✡ THE PROPOSAL

It was Christmas, 1919, and Bernard could not wait to leave the campus to get to Montreal. As he boarded the train to Montreal, he deposited his satchel on the floor beneath his feet, he settled down, closed his eyes, and began to mull over the present situation. He was sure of his love for Dora. That was a constant. He also knew that he was desperate to continue his education in order to achieve his long-term goals. But he knew he must secure a position that would help advance his career, whichever career that might be. It had to be something that challenged his intellect. He dreamed of becoming a university professor, but he had to face facts. First of all, a post-graduate degree would be mandatory. Second, was there any guarantee that the universities would be inclined to hire anyone Jewish? Not likely, no matter how highly qualified. But perhaps he could be one of the exceptions!

During his years spent in London, Bernard had been exposed to the appalling contrast between wealth and poverty. From that time on, Bernard had dreamed of a life serving humanity. He had begun by setting educational goals for himself so he could in turn educate others. However, no avenue had presented itself.

If only he would be awarded the graduate scholarships from either Cornell or Harvard for which he had applied. That would settle it. Without scholarships the financial hardships might be insurmountable, unless he exercised extreme parsimony.

Now, Dora. It was eight years since they first met. He remembered that experience as though it were yesterday. Demure young Dora, with her blonde wavy hair and sparkling blue eyes. He had felt immediately attracted to her. There was a serenity, a tranquillity that reached out to him and comforted him. Receptive yet reserved, she unobtrusively imbibed his opinions and his anecdotes. Later he had discovered her sense of humour and frivolity and the ease with which she interacted with others.

During the past three years, their feelings for each other had deepened. There was an unspoken understanding between them, but he had not yet said the four magic words. Did he have the right to ask her to wait another two years while he studied and then established himself in a position? Would it be fair to her? In addition, could his passionate nature tolerate two more years of waiting to be together? In most situations he considered himself to possess infinite patience - with his studies, in relationships with colleagues and friends - but he had to admit that being in love had placed limitations on his restraint. "Next stop, Montreal," the porter called out. He had not reached a firm decision. He would have to see how things turned out.

That evening they had no time alone. The family was seated around the dining room table and there was the usual chatter. Following dinner, as was their custom, they moved into the parlour where Ida sat at the piano. Rebecca sang a solo, followed by Dora, and then the others gathered round and joined in. It was the homelike atmosphere Bernard cherished.

The next day he and Dora arranged to go for a leisurely stroll together in Fletcher's Field at the base of Mount Royal. It was a beautiful, brisk, sunny afternoon. Bernard decided to present his dilemma to Dora. He opened up with re-iterating his quest for further education. He confessed that at the same time he was fed up with being apart from her, and expressed his wish to make a life with her. He avowed his deep and enduring love. But, he said, "How can I ask you to wait for me much longer, it isn't fair to you, is it?"

Dora had been listening intently to his dreams, his passion, and his dilemma. None of it was really new to her, except the part about marriage. Not that she had not guessed that he would propose to her eventually, but now that he had, she admitted to herself that she had been anticipating and eagerly awaiting this moment.

The first reassurance Bernard needed was that the deep love he felt for her was mutual. It was not easy for Dora to express her feelings, but she did manage to say, "Yes, of course, I do love you." As for waiting for him to complete further studies, she was encouraging.

"You mustn't worry, Bernard," she said, "if we are to spend the rest of our lives together, another year or two in the scheme of things, will not count that much. When the time is right, we'll make our plans. Weeks and months pass quickly. You mustn't torment yourself."

Should they tell the others? They decided it was premature, and that they would keep this delicious understanding between them. This was not a formal engagement - Bernard wanted to buy her a proper engagement ring and make a formal announcement. When they returned from their walk it was tea time, the family was gathered together, and it was obvious from the couple's radiant faces that something had transpired between them. For the moment, however, their privacy was respected and the family refrained from asking questions. But Dora's father, Samuel, opened a bottle of schnapps and the clinks of glasses were accompanied by a toast to life. *"L'chaim."*

Later, the sisters found it impossible to control themselves. They mounted the stairs, knocked on Dora's door, and invaded her bedroom bursting with questions. "Tell us, tell us, please, we won't tell, we promise."

"I shouldn't be telling you this, Bernard and I decided to keep it quiet."

"You can trust us. We are your sisters," they persisted. "Has he popped the question?" Dora nodded, trying not to show her elation. They jumped all over her, hugging and kissing her. "Lucky girl. He is a wonderful man. We love him dearly."

Bernard was not surprised nor was he displeased when Dora confessed that her sisters had "dragged" the story out of her. He was keenly aware of the bond that existed among them. And it was exciting to let them in on the secret. This was the first betrothal in the family.

After a rapturous holiday, the parting once more was sweet but sorrowful, as Bernard returned to his studies and Dora to her everyday routine at the Canadian Pacific office. But first, before unpacking or even having a cup of tea, Bernard dashed off a postcard announcing his safe arrival in Kingston. He addressed it to Dora's office at Windsor Station.

Jan. 5, 1920

Dearest Dodo.

After a monotonous journey of five hours, I have arrived here still alive. I feel tired, sleepy, blue, and so forth. Met many people on the way that I knew, but I spent most of the time all alone. Shall write to you soon.

S.B.H.

Although from the beginning Dora tried to keep her love life private, some of her colleagues noticed the frequent letters and postcards she received with postmarks from Kingston. One particular fellow delighted in teasing her about her "Kingston convict." Dora pretended to take offence, but it was all part of the game.

With the new understanding between them, they now corresponded with one another as befitted an engaged couple. Their greetings were even less formal than in the previous year. Dora adopted a nickname for Bernard, "Bernie," which she used from time to time. They continued to feed each other with their comings and goings, daily experiences and accomplishments. When her singing teacher, Mme. Laliberté, told Dora that she showed promise, Dora quoted to Bernard Mme. Laliberté's exact words. "Miss Ratner," Mme. said, looking exceedingly pleased with me, "I have detected a talent in you. It is called the talent of the climax, or the effect." Dora's friends and coleagues knew of her singing ability and she was invited to sing at social events. For example, when the C.P.R. hosted parties, Dora was expected to be one of the soloists.

Dear Bernie:

The program opened with a toast to the King and then another one to the
C.P.R. after which we proceeded with the supper. There was a long table and we were
45 in all. There was a name card for each one of us. The ladies (five in all) had their
names on a card attached to a flower. I had a fine rose, a gentleman on the left and
another gentleman on my right (not war time, is it?). While at the table they went on
with the musical program, which went off quite smoothly. I happened to pick out a
song that seemed to be liked. It was an old song published in 1902. It was written by
Gertrude Sans Souci. I found it in the house, I think you hardly ever heard me sing
it. It is entitled

WHEN SONG IS SWEET

Skies are only bright and fair
in your eyes of blue,
song is only sweet my dear
when I sing of you"
etc., etc...

This is how it starts. It is a very sentimental piece. My Irish friend gave a piano
solo, there were different speeches by various men, as for instance a gentleman
named Calder, who had accompanied the Prince of Wales, and some jokes by our
General Passenger Agent who is a very lively fellow. We also had a violinist who
entertained us by telling us some stories about the trenches. (He claims he used to
entertain the boys in the trenches with his fiddle.) Our poor boys (I mean our
returned soldiers, four in number) had a hard time controlling themselves, as he was
certainly exaggerating a great deal.

The evening ended with God Save the King and Auld Lang Syne. By this time I
was frozen, there was no heat in the room. It was twelve o'clock so we all got up
from the table and had a few dances. Everything sounds very good, but I wouldn't
like to tell you what happened to some of the men, they brought some scotch with
them and the result was that they had to be taken home.

This finishes my story for tonight. You poor boy, still with your exams on your
brain, I suppose, and I am worrying you with such a long letter, not a word more
then. Simply good-night and sweet dreams.

Dora

Jan 22, 1920
2 p.m.

Dear Dora:-

At last I am finis. At noon today I put the finishing touches to my last
examination paper, and believe me it was some relief to be through.

Many fellows have been studying much through the Christmas Holidays while I had a good time. Now I am glad: for I had both a good time and I think I did just as well at the examinations, as any of those who plugged through the holidays.

Our hockey team is going down to Montreal tomorrow afternoon to play McGill on Saturday. Gee, how I wish I could go with them! I hope, however, that Queen's boys will make mincemeat out of the McGill team. I expect they will give them a sound thrashing and show them who's who.

Good bye Sweetie. Be good.

Yours Bernard

Glorification of his team was short-lived. The outcome of the game provided Dora with the last laugh. Her footnote on January 24 read:

Hurrah for McGill! As usual, we won. Tell Abe he should come with them next time, then they would win.

Having to eat humble pie, Bernard was more charitable towards the McGill rugby team when they paid a visit to Kingston.

McGill Rugby team was here last Saturday. They are certainly a fine bunch of big husky fellows. They outplayed our boys from beginning to end and the victory they fully deserve. Queen's boys are much lighter and therefore a number of casualties on our side took place. I watched the game and it was surely a treat to see it.

In the hiatus between exams, Bernard could now also catch up on his letter writing. During his visits to Montreal, he had often delighted in teasing Ida, Dora's "kid sister." She seemed to enjoy it. On this last visit she pouted that he never wrote any letters specifically addressed to her. So, feeling in good humour, he decided to tease her about her students, her piano teacher, Alfred Laliberté, and to throw in a few provocative remarks about marriage.

Queen's University
Kingston, Ontario
January 24, 1920

Hello H'Ida!

How is the g(h)irl? I just feel in a good mood tonight, and in the right humor to write letters to all my sweethearts. So you are one of the victims of my good humor. Comprenez-vous?

At noon Thursday when I put my seal to the last examination paper, I began to feel finally permitted to enjoy the fragrant breezes of the wide atmosphere, and to inhale the fresh air of the open fields.

I should have celebrated the happy occasion with a dose of something strong but lo! I live in a dry province and the luxuries of wicked Quebec are not to be touched by the saints of Ontario. Besides, it would not do to become too tipsy-topsy, for Thursday evening I was down to dinner to one of the profs and so of course the least I could do was to be sober.

Well how are you getting along and how are your pupils? I miss your music very much. One night last week while I was hard at work reviewing some notes for the next examination, I heard the piano go off, as never before. I knew it was not the girl in the house playing, for I am quite used to her banging the keys. It must have been some visitor with a soul as well as fingers to play. I felt like inventing some excuse to go down to the parlor. But I was not in presentable attire, and had to stay where I was.

When "Tell Me Why Nights are Lonesome" etc. was played I could no more concentrate my mind on my notes. I closed the book for a while, balanced my chair on the two hind legs, and put my feet on the table. I was like this for nearly half an hour meditating, closing and opening my eyes, and dreaming of days gone by. (Abe and Harry were studying in the other room and therefore did not see me in this position. I never told them about it either.)

Suddenly I woke up, looked at the watch, it was nearly 10:30 which meant I could study that evening only three and a half more hours. So I hastened to my prosaic work until the Land of Nod closed the evening's episode.

Does Laliberté still indulge in calling his scholars "rascals"? If he does I'll be around soon to challenge him for a duel. I presume it is married life that makes him cranky. Bachelors are usually angels, until they make the mistake of their lives by getting married. You will surely agree with me in this, won't you? Poor fellow, he used to be happy as a single man - always nice, kind, gentle, sweet, innocent, and pleasant. Now he is married and as a result he is always bad, unkind, rough, cruel, miserable, unpleasant, and a rascal. Some change! Poor chap. All on account of a girl. I shall have to look out and be more careful. Don't you think?

Seeing the thrill on Ida's face when she received the letter from Bernard, Dora was pleased. A letter such as this offered some humourous relief from Ida's worries of finding employment. Although she and Annie had graduated with honours from Macdonald College, they were not having an easy time finding full-time employment in the Protestant School Board. They were resigned to being hired only temporarily as substitute teachers.

"Jewish girls who chose the teaching profession were admitted into Macdonald College from which they graduated with honors, but not one of them was accepted by the Protestant Board, while English girls of lesser scholastic standing were assured of positions even before graduation."

Bernard Figler, in his Biography of Louis Fitch

The sisters persevered, and Annie landed a position at Springfield Park School at $60.00 a month. It was very far from the family home, but she was thrilled. Meanwhile Dora knew that Annie's male counterparts out West were earning twice that amount. Two summers earlier Abe Friedgut had written that he was earning $100.00 a month - and expecting a raise - at a school in Edenwold, Saskatchewan, 16 miles from Regina. Bernard, in Jasmin, earned the same amount. But Dora's family's enthusiasm was not dampened. They were keenly aware that being a Jewish female, Annie was fortunate to obtain a teaching job at all. Ida, too, was fortunate. Providentially for her, a number of teachers were ill at Alexandria School in downtown Montreal. A rotating teacher was urgently needed as temporary replacement. Between teaching there and giving private piano lessons, the ambitious young woman was doing extremely well financially. Before long she had saved enough money to purchase the "Hudson Seal coat" she had seen advertised for $250.00 in *The Montreal Star* by the The Alex Nelson Com., The Old Reliable Furriers, at 380 St. Catherine West.

Meanwhile Annie's teaching position at Springfield Park had another serious drawback. Besides being far from home, the classroom situation was far from ideal. It was February, the height of winter, and there were mountains of snow on the streets of Montreal. Never mind the problems she encountered travelling to the school herself, but once arriving at the school she was unable to warm up. The school had run out of coal and was freezing cold. The trucks could not get through the snow to deliver a new supply. Annie was stricken with frostbite. The children were also freezing. But this was her job, and a teaching one at that. She treated her frostbite on the weekend and come Monday morning, soldiered on. Dora and her family could not imagine how the children fared under such adverse conditions. Annie said that some parents kept their children at home.

At this stage Samuel, Dora's father, was naturally optimistic that his daughters, now of marrying age, would be wedded before long. Wasn't the house always filled with young men courting the girls? So he ordered "a frock suit" and told them that he "is ready" for hint, hint, special events. Samuel could not know then that the returns on his investment would be limited. He would get to wear that suit to only two weddings out of eight possibilities.

In the interval, Bernard had received the results of his final examinations and, as usual, had achieved "highest standing." With graduation imminent, and with the War ended, he decided it would be to his advantage to apply for naturalization papers. He wrote Dora about it. She promptly advised him that now was a propitious time to shorten his name. Never mind that the name Haltrecht had a significant family history that dated back to the mid-eighteenth century. Never mind that every person with this name was a descendant of the then-famous Rabbi R. Noah ben R. Shimon whose written works had been published under the title of *Toldas Noah* (the writings of Noah), and which would later be placed in the Hebrew University archives in Jerusalem.

Dora, seemingly unaware of these details and the depth of attachment Bernard had to his surname, suggested that this name might become an "obstacle" later on. Did she think an identifiable Jewish name would invite anti-Semitism, or did she simply consider the name too cumbersome for North Americans to spell and/or pronounce? Had she been referring to potential prejudice, her ideas would have foreshadowed the feelings of some of the British Haltrecht cousins. These family members, notwithstanding the historical significance of the name, would shorten (to Hall) and in some cases, even change their names (to Howard) following the Second World War. They hoped that Anglicization of the name would circumvent the anti-Semitism so prevalent in Britain at the time.

When Bernard recounted to Dora the historical significance of his family name, she realized this was a sensitive topic, and acquiesced at once, speedily dropping the topic of surnames.

Three years earlier Bernard had written to Dora for her opinion about his first name. She had replied:

I have to laugh when I think of your postscript, i.e. whether I like the name of Bernard better than your other two names. Well, it certainly does puzzle me. I could not actually understand your sudden question. What difference does a name make? You know that it is the person who bears the name that counts.

However, if you really want my opinion, for the sake of argument I would like to disagree with you. I cannot help admitting that Bernard, as a name (we are discussing about names only) sounds sort of revered, somebody one can look up to. Bernard or Boris are equally nice.

Of course I have nothing absolutely against your other names!

13 ✡ 1920

Dora was in hospital with acute appendicitis. She had been trying to keep the episode from Bernard so that he would not worry, but her sisters did not cooperate. Rachel, in particular, thought he had a right to know, especially if surgery was indicated. As soon as Dora was feeling better, she wrote to Bernard.

Montreal, March 4, 1920

Dear Bernie:-

Good Purim! Did you eat *Homentashen*? I did not. I wanted to write you on Thursday and then break the news on the state of my health. I absolutely made Rae promise me faithfully that she should not write to you, but it seems she did not keep her promise. I was just told by Rebecca that you phoned last night and that makes it all clear to me. I shall certainly not forgive her this act. I wanted to keep this from you, as you have enough things to worry about just now. However, it's done.

I suppose she wrote to you the whole story. I shall not start all over again, besides I am writing this lying flat on my back, which makes it very uncomfortable. I am feeling much better this morning. In fact Dr. Archibald was here to see me yesterday and said that there was absolutely no danger now. I need no operation unless I really want to get rid of the appendix for good, but I told him that I would sooner be treated medically instead of surgically. I therefore should be able to go home in a couple of days which means, I presume, by Saturday.

There is no need for you to be anxious or worry. The pain has nearly subsided. I have normal temperature. The nurse remarked to me this morning while taking my temperature that I am a fake, as it was absolutely normal. One of the handsome doctors is absolutely disappointed as he was sure I was going to have an operation. But who cares! They can all be disappointed if they like. PLEASE DON'T WORRY.

Adieu, Good health for both of us.

Dora

Somewhat relieved, Bernard posted a tender, intimate and consoling letter to Dora directly to the hospital. Then he carried on with his studies, anxiously awaiting news of her progress, and hopefully her release from the hospital. The day of her release arrived under unexpected dramatic circumstances.

Mar. 7, 1920

Dear Bernie:-

Your last letter found me at the RVH [Royal Victoria Hospital], that is, Saturday morning, and I only went home in the afternoon. The weather was dreadful. It was so stormy that the ambulance could not come up for me but with great difficulty I managed to get home in a closed sleigh. From the sleigh Maxie and Issie had to carry me up to the house in their arms. Your strong muscular arms would have come in handy then. Don't you wish you were here?

The next day Rebecca read to Dora *The Montreal Star*'s report of the unpredicted snowstorm. It began with the headline:

WEATHER MAN AS FICKLE AS WOMAN
Saturday, March 6, 1920

The weatherman is in capricious mood again. Within the last twenty-four hours Montreal has had sun, rain, sleet, slop, snow, and ordinary gray weather. From a mild sunny morning which looked like spring itself yesterday, the afternoon and evening developed into mid-winter and a snowstorm of the worst kind.

This morning the citizens of Outremont, Westmount and other outlying places had to dig themselves out of the snowbanks. The gale which blew during the night has piled the snow in great banks which make some of the side streets well nigh impassable...

Until snow came Montreal was at the stage when drivers of horse vehicles did not know whether to use sleigh or wheel carriage...

Dear Bernard:-

This is Sunday. I am still in bed. Am learning to get up today, but it is very hard. I am attempting to write, but I have to rest after each line, as my arm is very weak. I do not feel any pains now, but I am weak. The weather is beautiful today. The sun is shining very brightly into my window It was very sweet of you to enclose that little violet. I always like violets as they have such a beautiful meaning - love. Could anyone wish for anything more? No.

Dora

P.S. Don't you think this is a long letter for an invalid like me?

Dora began what she expected to be the gradual recuperation from her illness. At first, all indications seemed normal. The following week, while holding on to Rebecca's arm, she managed to slowly walk the few blocks outdoors from the house to City Hall Avenue and back. It was a glorious day, the sun was shining and it was warmer than usual for this time of year. When they returned to the house, Rebecca left for the library, and Dora decided to rest a little on the veranda. It was too nice to go inside. After a while her French-Canadian next-door neighbour came out of his house and noticed her reclining there.

"Oh, Miss Ratner, I am so happy to see that you are better," he said. "My wife and I were just talking about you at lunch today and wondering when we would see you back on your feet. You gave us quite a scare. But never mind, it's such a beautiful day, why don't I take you for a little walk?"

"Oh, thank you," Dora answered, "but I have already been for a little walk with my sister, Rebecca."

"Another little walk won't do you any harm, in fact, it will be good for you. Please let me have the honour of walking with you. I'll take good care of you."

"But you are on your way to work, aren't you. If I go with you, you mustn't desert me on the way."

"What are you saying? Of course not," he replied.

So, taking her arm in a mockingly gallant fashion, they strolled, this time just to St. Denis Street, and back to the house. This was enough for one day. Dora, pleased with her progress, but feeling fatigued by this time, went into the house to recuperate from the exercise.

Bernard, meantime, was so anxious to see Dora that he could no longer contain himself. College exams notwithstanding, he arranged to take the train to Montreal for the weekend. Dora, buoyed by her progress and the anticipation of his visit, was taking good care of herself so that she could surprise him by meeting him at the station. When he arrived and saw her face, albeit a little pale, he was thrilled.

All weekend he treated her delicately like a fragile recuperating invalid. But she insisted she was almost back to normal, and the first two days of his visit they took leisurely walks to Parc Lafontaine where they sat on a bench and watched the skaters. On the third day, Sunday, Bernard accepted her parents' offer to borrow their car. Tucking her in with a warm wool blanket on the passenger seat beside him, he drove her north to the Laurentian Mountains where they stopped at a small inn for hot chocolate and dessert, returning just in time for the family dinner. In the evening they relaxed in their usual manner. Loath to leave, but at least satisfied that she was well on the road to recovery, Bernard returned to Kingston and his studies.

Mar 22, 1920 (1:30 p.m.)

Dear Dora:-

I can assure you I don't feel as happy now as I felt twenty-four hours ago. Yesterday this time we had just come back from the mountains and were ready to sit down for dinner. Now I am sitting in my room meditating over the recent past and considering how cruel time is: forcing everything to have a beginning and an end.

After a monotonous and miserable journey of five hours, I finally reached my place of abode in Kingston at four o'clock this morning. The train was late as usual. I found the house in darkness and silence. Everything and everyone was asleep. I put the lights on and found my two mates in the Land of Nod. They did not hear me at all, for I tried to be as quiet as a mouse. At 4:30 I went to bed.

At 7:15 Abe woke me up and I had to dress immediately to get to an eight o'clock lecture, which was a real nuisance. The first question of his as soon as I opened my eyes was "How is Dora?" He did not ask me how I enjoyed the week-end for he knew the answer beforehand.

I have so many things to attend to to-day that I must shorten this letter. I wish you to be cheerful all the time. Please let not little things worry you, and do not take everything to heart. Eat, drink and be merry. Will you do this? If you do it you will get stronger every day, and this is what you should see to.

I need hardly mention how happy I was to be with you for the last three days, but all good things as a rule are short lived. However, we must be satisfied for the little we get and hope for greater things in the future. No doubt time will fly and we shall be together again.

Good bye, dear,

Bernard

But then, unbeknownst to Bernard, an unexpected relapse occurred and Dora was forced back to bed. The family was once more confronted with the possibility of surgery for Dora and with it, the accompanying risk of infection. Sterilization and antiseptics could reduce the risk, but if an infection did develop, there was little treatment a doctor could offer. Bernard had not received Dora's customary response to his letter, and after a few days he became disconsolate and anxious.

Dear Dora:-

    I cannot make out why I have not heard from you all week. Day after day I call at the post office for mail, and each time I have to turn back feeling "blue." I hope everything is well with you, and that I shall receive a letter from you before this reaches you. In the meantime I feel quite impatient and can hardly wait any longer.

    Be a good girl and write immediately. Regards to all.

Bernard

Mar 26, 1920

Dear Bernard:-

    I received your letter on Tuesday morning and intended to answer it the next day, but fortune turned against me. I took sick on Tuesday evening. Dr Fraser was here on Wednesday and sent for Dr Archibald who came up to see me last night,

    After some deliberation, he decided that this was not an attack on the appendix after all, but an inflammation of the bowels and there is no necessity for an operation.

    I feel much better today, so you have no reason to worry about me. I know you are busy and I am sorry to worry you with trifles. I shall curtail this letter now as I find it inconvenient to write in bed. Be patient and expect the best.

Dora

P.S. Thank you for inquiring about me.

    Now Dora had to accept the fact that it would take several weeks before she would be able to return to work or to her lectures at McGill. And she was forced to postpone her travel plans to New York.

    I had no idea at all that I was going to get sick. I planned to go to New York, as I wrote you, to buy some spring clothes and therefore have not a new thing to wear. You will have to like me in my old clothes, so far anyway.

    Fortunately, Rebecca was in the same classes, so they studied together from Rebecca's notes, Dora propped up by pillows in her cozy bed. Rebecca, a natural scholar, enjoyed filling her in. Dora was particularly concerned about the three lectures she missed on Argumentation. Rebecca took on the role of tutor, easily reiterating the professor's discourse on the topic. Still Dora, not expecting to pass, did not let on to Bernard that she even planned to take the examinations. She was still feeling weak, and could predict what his advice would be. When the day arrived, the family, especially her parents, still extremely concerned about her health, were strongly opposed to her going out. But Dora argued with them. "I'll be all right," she insisted. "Rebecca will be with me the whole time."

The results were announced promptly, and to her surprise, she had passed. Both sisters received their certificates. Excited about her accomplishment, Dora jokingly referred to their certificates as their "degrees."

Dora admired university graduates, especially women. Very few women she knew had earned BA degrees. Even the most enlightened families considered choice professions for women to be teachers, nurses, or librarians. One did not need a degree for these professions and in any case, these professions would be temporary, only lasting until the daughters married, after which they would be occupied with domestic duties and charity work. So Dora and Rebecca contented themselves over the years with taking evening courses at McGill. This way they selected the specific courses that interested them, and they could take as few or as many as they wished within a given year. And, in the meantime, they were earning a living, enabling them to live comfortably.

While Dora was enjoying her small educational success, Bernard, during this interim, had received bitterly disappointing news from Cornell. He had been counting on obtaining a scholarship, but instead he received a polite rejection letter. What had gone wrong? His Economics and History professors at Queen's (Dean Skelton and Professor Black) had been very encouraging about his chances and had written glowing letters of support for his application. This was a cruel blow, not only to his ego, but also to his dream of graduate school.

Well, maybe it was not meant to be. It was time to put Dora first. She needed his support. During his financial hardships as an undergraduate at Queen's she was continuously offering to help him financially. She kept entreating him to be "frank" with her and let her know if he needed any money. She told him that she was earning good wages and always had money put aside. Too proud to accept in any case, he was fortunately able to manage on his own, but he felt the time had come for him to look after her.

The Ratner family wanted to make sure that Bernard ate properly, especially at Passover time when they knew that he could not obtain kosher food at the college cafeteria. The thought that he might be forced to eat *treyf* was inconceivable to them. He was not in the habit of letting them know that he had abandoned kosher eating years ago and enjoyed a variety of foods forbidden in the Jewish religion. They constantly sent him parcels of goodies. At this particular holiday time, they had packed up so much food for him (meals to last eight days) that Dora advised him to take along a muscular classmate to the post office. The box was too large and too heavy for one person to manage. Their nurturing was most appreciated by Bernard, but now his concern was looking after Dora.

Apr 8, 1920

Dear Dora:-

If I can get a good, permanent, paying position, I may drop entirely the idea of going in for further studies for a more advanced degree. I hate to see you having to go back to work. I should like to see you quit work altogether as soon as possible. I am going to try for a position with some large industrial concern, and wait patiently. This is all I can do just now.

April 10. 1920

Dear Bernie:-

I was indeed very sorry to hear that you did not get your scholarship from Cornell. Do not feel downhearted. If you decide to go you will go anyhow. One year does not mean so much. You may earn enough during the summer to put you through. Besides I do not expect to be sick all the time. If I do not earn enough during the summer I shall get well and work next winter and therefore help you out.

I had my fortune told and it said that I am going to be very rich and happy and that a dark young man who is a very dear friend of mine is going to have his wish fulfilled and will make my future. I wonder if you know the young man. Do you know what else the cards said - that a dark girl is very much interested in that dark young man. This made me feel jealous of course and I shall have to look out for that dark girl. I was also told that a fair young man is interested in me. What do you think of that? We are even now, aren't we? It is all nonsense, is it not?

By April 15, 1920, Dora had returned to work to hear from her boss how much she was missed. The chief clerk assured her that he had never kept a job open for such a long time for "any girl." She was flattered. With her health restored, she began to apply herself to help Bernard find a summer or permanent job in Montreal.

Perhaps you could take a letter of recommendation from one of your professors to President Beatty of the CPR, seeing he is Chancellor of Queen's.

At last Bernard not only graduated Queen's with a BA *cum honoribus* but also won the Gowan scholarship in Economics. Although he had not received the scholarship to Cornell, he was accepted at Harvard as a graduate student in History. His bio in the Queen's Year Book described his background and his peers' impressions of him.

S. B. HALTRECHT

Bernie heard the call of his Alma Mater while teaching on the prairies of Saskatchewan. He registered for Extra-Mural study and in January 1917, appeared in the halls of Queen's, joining Arts '20. Ambitious, energetic and devoted to his work, he was at once recognized as a valuable asset to his year, which he served creditably on various occasions.

In his junior year he filled the position of Orator on the Executive and debated successfully in the preliminaries for the inter-year championship. This year he is the popular chancellor of the Arts '20 exchequer and one of the active members of the Year Book Committee. Bernie was not known for his prowess on the athletic field, but he was admired and respected for his sound arguments and sane judgment. As he goes forth into the world to perform his task he takes with him the good wishes of the year, who will remember him as a sincere friend and worthy student.

Bernard knew if he stayed out West he could quite easily secure employment. But Bernard was fed up with being practical. How much longer could he and Dora stand being apart? Yet he did not want to raise Dora's hopes. How could he risk going to Montreal with no prospects of employment? The Ratner family inquired about positions for him. But while he was in Kingston, unavailable for interviews, the affair was difficult. Letters flew back and forth between him and Dora about potential summer employment. None of his options was remotely the grandiose full-time position Bernard was seeking.

Finally, with no assurance at all of either summer or permanent work, Bernard sent off his trunk to Montreal not specifying to Dora that he would soon follow. Dora, thrilled with the news of the dispatch of the trunk, took it as a hopeful, even definitive sign.

April 20, 1920

Your trunk came yesterday, which means that you will follow it, isn't that right?

When the train, this time with Bernard on it, arrived in Montreal, the family was at the station to greet him and take him to their home. The euphoria was only mitigated by the fact that no job had presented itself. But a number of interviews had been set up for him.

As luck would have it, he was not forced to accept any unappealing positions. Ida, teaching at Aberdeen School, discovered that the Summer Schools were amalgamating and looking for a principal to assume a supervisory position. Bernard, who was already known at Aberdeen, was offered the position. He thus became the first principal of the Summer Recreational Schools, the forerunner of today's summer urban camps. Although not his immediate goal of a permanent position, he readily accepted it, knowing this hiatus would give him a "window" to look around for something more permanent.

During the summer, the Ratner family, as was their custom, spent the summer in the country. Lac Marois, with its tranquil setting in the Laurentian Mountains, some 40 miles from Montreal, was a restful spot. Family members would journey to Shawbridge by train, then take a horse and carriage to the Lake. The easy accessibility would give Bernard the opportunity to make the trip up north to enjoy weekends with Dora. Weekdays they would keep in touch by daily postcards. Whoever was going to Shawbridge would drop in at the post office to deliver and/or post mail.

POSTCARD

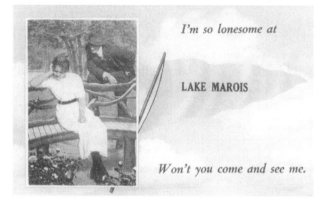

I'm so lonesome at

LAKE MAROIS

Won't you come and see me.

33 St. Louis Square
Montreal
July 20, 1920

Miss D. Ratner
Shawbridge, Que.
Dear "Girlie,"

Sorry I could not write to you till now. Every minute of the day as well as evening was taken up. We had a most successful picnic. About 1500 children were present and all of them (as well as the teachers) were taken home in automobiles. The "Pathe" took moving pictures of the whole affair and they will be shown in all the movie houses in the city. The Mount Royal School won the boys' cup, and the Aberdeen School won the girls' cup. The excitement was tremendous and the children shouted themselves hoarse. Will see all of you Friday.

By by   Bernie

Meanwhile Bernard's sister, Anna, persisted in trying to convince Bernard to find work in London so that she could have him near her. At second best, she wanted to help him advance himself. So she flaunted her own contacts, most likely achieved through her husband, Edmond, the professor of languages, who, from his office on Oxford Street, had tutored some impressive people, royalty included.

415 Oxford St

London W. 1

July 3rd, 1920

My dear Sallie:-

I read your letter and all the enclosures beaming with delight. Yes, Sallie, Thank God! You have done well. How much I feel with you and delight with you in your great <u>Success</u>. It is such a great Triumph.

And there is still another triumph, you have grown so big and strong and you look so well. By your photograph you look about 6 ft, but you must let me know your exact height and weight. You remember Sallie, you were once my little brother and now I can only claim to be your little sister. What a tremendous change!! And yet, I can sincerely assure you I would not have it otherwise. The only thing is that I miss you very much. I should like you to be near me, naturally.

Again the greatest and most important of all things now is to get a good and remunerative position so that you could settle down comfortably and with prospects to further developments in the future. Now would you like to tell me all your plans and very fully.

I went to see my friend, Miss Black, yesterday (you met her at my school, I believe) and I told her all about you. She is a great friend of Sir Gregory and Lady Foster. Sir Gregory Foster is the Provost of the London University, and the head of the Educational World in England. He is a very great authority on most important matters. Perhaps you have heard of him. He is also very well known on the other side of the Atlantic.

Were you here I could have easily secured an introduction for you, and no doubt he would have been able to help you, but as it is, I have asked Miss Black to write to Sir Gregory and ask his advice where you would have greater scope for advancement, by remaining in Canada or coming over here. He knows the Educational centres in Canada and also in the United States. He often goes backwards and forwards on important state missions.

And now, Sallie, write to me. My fondest love, Good Luck and God Bless you

Yours ever

Anna

Bernard had wished to be an academic, but to achieve this goal he would have had to continue to graduate school. He did have an acceptance from Harvard but that would mean further separation from Dora. Eight years of correspondence and of living in separate cities - they had had enough of that. Also to be considered was the unlikelihood of a Jewish graduate securing a university professorship. For example, even as recently as 1978, when Queen's University became a secular institution, the following proviso was added: "... the University shall continue distinctively Christian and the trustees shall satisfy themselves of the Christian character of those appointed to the teaching staff."

Not until 1981 was the proviso dropped.

Fortuitously, before long, word was out that the Canadian Jewish Congress was forming an organization called the Jewish Immigrant Aid Society (JIAS) and that they were looking for a young, dynamic, and educated person to run it. Surely this was a splendid opportunity. Bernard needed no coaxing. He applied for the position and secured an interview with the search committee, which consisted of prominent Jewish community leaders.

Bernard waited on tenterhooks for some form of notification. At last it came in the form of an informal telephone call. "Well, Mr. Haltrecht," the chairman of the committee said, "Congratulations. The Board unanimously decided that you are our preferred candidate. We'll expect to see you at our next meeting a week from Monday."

Hallelujah! He had landed the job. Now Bernard not only held a permanent position, but more important, a prestigious and challenging one, one through which he could make an important contribution to the community. The time was ripe for him and Dora to make real plans. With his earnings from the summer job, he would be able to save enough money to buy Dora a diamond engagement ring with a matching wedding band for later. In the fall, ensconced in the new job, Bernard placed the ring on Dora's finger and the engagement became official. Parties were organized, the date was set for February 8, 1921, and the engraved wedding invitations were ordered. These few months would give out-of-town guests sufficient time to make plans for the trip to Montreal.

Mr. & Mrs. U. Ratner

request the honor of your presence at the marriage reception of their daughter

Dorothy

to

S. B. Haltrecht

on Tuesday, February the Eighth
nineteen hundred and twenty-one

at 8 o'clock

33 St. Louis Square, Montreal

Since the Ratner home was spacious, easily accommodating the required number of people, and fitted with electricity, it was the natural choice of venue for the wedding reception. On the day of the big event the guests arrived and were ushered into the parlour to await the bride and groom, who would make their dramatic appearance. When Ida began to play the wedding march, the bride and groom descended the steep winding stairs. Dora, in a beautiful white satin beaded gown with matching headdress, looked radiant. Bernard, in tails and top hat, looked suitably elegant. When the couple reached the parlour, Rebecca gave

ST. LOUIS SQUARE

a rendition of "Oh Promise Me" in her beautiful coloratura voice. Dora did not wish to sing at her own wedding.

There had been lengthy discussions about where the couple should honeymoon. Together they pored over brochures and advertisements in the paper. Finally Bernard and Dora decided on a place to honeymoon. They would make the trip to Lakewood, New Jersey. It sounded like a romantic spot. Next, a place to live. As luck would have it, a house at 258 St. Louis Square posted a *Maison à Louer* sign. It was right across the Square from the family - just the ideal location to begin a new chapter in their lives.

II

SETTING DOWN ROOTS

14 ✿ JEWISH IMMIGRANT AID SOCIETY (JIAS)

In the aftermath of the First World War, a flood of homeless people in Central and Eastern Europe, desperate to emigrate, urgently needed to find a haven that could offer peace and safety. The World War had affected all people and the European Jews were no exception. Their plight became a major concern to Jews in the rest of the world. In Canada immigration was placed first on the Jewish community's agenda. In the minds of the Canadian Jewish Congress leaders, Canada was a natural choice to welcome Jewish immigrants. Jews had been pouring into the country during the previous two decades, and most of them were now well-established. Canadian Jews felt it their moral responsibility to help their own less fortunate compatriots to have access to better lives. Someone had to meet the war-weary, battered immigrants at the ports and stations across the country to offer them the required advice and protection, as well as to provide them with any legal and other assistance that they might require.

On June 30, 1920, delegates from a number of Jewish organizations met and founded the Jewish Immigrant Aid Society of Canada (JIAS) to service close to 6,000 Jewish immigrants who would be passing through the Quebec port from the following April to November. Its first executive consisted of leading members of the Jewish community. Mr. Louis Fitch, lawyer and Vice-President of the Canadian Jewish Congress (C.J.C.), President; Mr. H.M. Caiserman, General Secretary of the C.J.C., General Secretary; Rabbi Hirsch Cohen, Treasurer; and Messrs B. Goldstein and L. Lewis ex officio, representatives of the Jewish Colonization Association (J.C.A.)

In the autumn of the same year, Bernard was appointed director of the Montreal headquarters of JIAS, which generated branches in other major Canadian cities, including Toronto and Winnipeg, and he was given the authority to take full charge of the administration. His job was to organize and consolidate the work of the Society both in Montreal and at the ports. Intrinsically well organized, passionate about his convictions, dedicated to his work, and deeply compassionate by nature, he was the ideal person to administer this organization. His ability to communicate with people of varying classes and educational levels, his mediating skills, and his perseverance under adverse conditions were all characteristics that would be essential in this post. It could fulfil his dream of making a difference.

He told Dora, and he announced publicly, that he foresaw JIAS as being a "monument in Canadian Jewish history." When he visited the Ratners' home, Dora and her family would listen intently to him talk of the immigrants' dire situation, of the crucial work being carried out by JIAS, and of his personal mission to do everything in his power to help. The sisters in particular were strongly community minded, and so were filled with admiration for Bernard's leadership role in such a noble undertaking. Dora was not only thrilled with his new status, but also liked being financially secure.

On his first day, Bernard set up a system for the administration of the Society. Before long JIAS moved into an office shared by the Mizrachi and Canadian Jewish Congress on the top floor of the Molson building. Soon afterwards the floor was filled with people and luggage, and one day the Molson's Bank Building manager and a burly assistant stormed into the office and, in no uncertain terms, told the startled inhabitants that they would have to move out. Although Bernard was incensed at the abrasive manner in which the assistant had behaved to these dispossessed people, he calmed the immigrants by reassuring them that this was a temporary obstacle and that the problem would be solved.

In the next few days Bernard worked feverishly to solve the dilemma. He was constantly on the telephone and in emergency meetings describing the urgent situation and explaining the need for an immediate solution. He urged the influential Board of Directors who had various types of connections in the city to help. To the relief of all concerned, they came through with an empty store at 900 St. Lawrence Boulevard. This place would at least serve as office space for the time being.

The Society, with Bernard at its helm, had its work cut out for it. Jewish immigration into Canada quickly assumed considerable proportions and the Canadian government began to institute rigorous restrictions. New arrivals were being detained and were in danger of being deported back to the very countries from which they had finally escaped almost certain death. Requests for help were coming in from all over North America from relatives of those detained. The office was flooded with telegrams and long-distance calls, and the staff reciprocated in kind. Appeals had to be made on behalf of all these frantic people.

The present headquarters could no longer accommodate the necessary expansion of space and staff. In November 1920, the Board of Directors purchased a three-storey building at 725 Notre Dame Street West. This building became the new headquarters. It could now meet the Society's needs, which included space not only for administration and meetings, but also sufficient space for an immigrants' shelter.

This meant that those new arrivals who had no place to go would now have a place to rest their heads - in the shelter's dormitories. In addition, they would have access to a kitchen and showers. There were congratulations all round - but unfortunately premature. Bernard pictured the 300 refugees being held at the Quebec port, some of whom had been held there for months. He remembered his own experience arriving in Canada and his anxiety when he saw the DETAINED sign stamped in huge letters on his release form. To this day, he did not know why he had been initially rejected, but he knew he had been fortunate.

The thought of these immigrants, many families and many young children, some in ill health, being detained for three months in deplorable conditions, not knowing whether they would eventually be allowed into the country, caused him sleepless nights. He envisioned their situation, confined in a dimly-lit enormous warehouse shed, herded like cattle to unpalatable, unsanitary meals, and separated from their loved ones. He empathized with their despair and demoralization. Fourteen had already been sent back to Europe, creating panic among the others. Something had to be done quickly.

The Montreal headquarters pressured the Canadian government. In the winter of 1921, the Port of Quebec closed and the several hundred detained were released to Montreal. At the same time, the Port of St. John opened and boats began to arrive there as well as Halifax, bringing many more immigrants.

Meanwhile, there was increasing political resistance to Jewish immigrants who were described by the federal government as belonging to "races that cannot be assimilated without social or economic loss to Canada." British and American citizens were not considered a threat to the Canadian way of life because their "racial characteristics" were similar to the Anglo-Canadian majority, placing them in the "Preferred Group." So while these immigrants were welcomed into the country, obstacles were frequently placed in the Jewish immigrants' paths.

First, many of these immigrants were rejected for non-compliance with "technicalities" of the Immigrant Act. Inspectors, at their own whim, could decide who was to pass through and who was to remain. And they did not have to inform the rejected immigrant of the reason for the rejection. Being kept in ignorance only compounded the fear and anxiety.

Second, all detainees were forced to pay the federal government for room and board while detained, and the steamship companies were being held liable for any immigrants who were shipped back without having paid the required amounts. The steamship companies in turn were demanding cash deposits of $20 per person - an astronomical sum for destitute Eastern Europeans, especially those with large families. Otherwise, they would be immediately deported.

JIAS undertook the financial commitment, but before long the bills of the steamship companies reached over $10,000. Where was the money to come from? A cross-Canada campaign was held in April 1921 to appeal for funds and membership. By this time, JIAS had also established a Legal Bureau in Ottawa to look after appeal cases. And the federal government had been persuaded to pass an Order-in-Council to disseminate information to European Jews not to leave their countries without being assured that they had passed all the regulations of the Immigrant Act. It was imperative they know that the doors of Canada were not necessarily open to them.

The Canadian government attempted to warn European Jews that they were not necessarily welcome in Canada, but the information did not disseminate quickly enough. The first two boatloads of 253 Jews arriving at the Port of Quebec in early September discovered that only 50 percent of them were acceptable. Of the 269 Jewish passengers who arrived on the third boat in mid-September, 170 were rejected.

Although rumours persisted in Europe that it might not be so easy to immigrate, many Jews, desperate to leave the abhorrent conditions to which they were subjected, believed they had to give it a chance. They only listened to accounts of the numbers who had successfully immigrated, fostering hope that they would be among those who would make it. Tragically, when the fourth boat docked in Halifax, all 156 passengers were rejected and ordered deported. The pleas of those detained were heartbreaking. Their voices rang in Bernard's ears. An agile and enterprising passenger of the *Saxonia*, desperate to get a message through to his family in Quebec City, shinnied up a pipe and tossed a message encased in a bottle into the harbour. The message read:

Brothers! Remember the issue. It is a question of life and death for men, women, and children, who in coming to this country hoped to establish for themselves a quiet and restful home. If we are sent home we have nothing left to do but to throw ourselves into the ocean. Remember that Petlura, Deniken, Balachovitch and others have already thrown into the sea enough of our brothers, sisters, mothers, fathers, and little children. Do not be a party to such a tragedy, for on you lies the duty to help us.

Bernard was determined that these immigrants would not be sent back to the hell from which they had barely escaped with their lives. His office, together with the Ottawa bureau, worked feverishly to find some other country that would receive them. At last Cuba agreed to allow the deportees to enter their country. Negotiations with steamship lines took place, and in the meantime, the Department of Immigration ordered a re-examination of the immigrants. Those who complied were admitted under special permits.

On the great historic day when a large number of immigrants were released from jail and saved from the horrible fate of deportation, 47 of them signed the following letter expressing their thanks to the Canadian Jewish community. The letter was hand delivered to the office and Bernard opened it.

On this day of our release, we the undersigned, take the opportunity to express to you the warmest thanks from the depths of our souls. No words or phrases can describe the feeling of the freed man towards his liberator. Our Jewish history is almost fully covered with blood and tears, and anywhere the Jew has trespassed, a mysterious power would lead that country to prosperity and the Jew to desolation.

The only place on earth on this globe, that is - thank Heaven - not yet acquainted with the horrible events that happened to other lands of our *goluth* [exile], is that of Canada and the United States, and when the doors of Canada were about to be closed upon us and we were about to be deported back to Europe, with nothing to greet us there but suffering, the only ray of hope which gleamed on us was extinguished and a Jewish community of old and young men, women and children were about to be crushed.

Therefore, our kind liberators, we would ask you to accept the only means with which we can thank you, that is our blessings from the depth of our hearts which we hope will reach the gates of Heaven and be sanctioned by the Almighty.

Bernard was moved to tears. He never minded or complained about the long hours, the perpetual workload, the continual anxiety that required his complete energies. For this dedication he expected no official recognition or reward. It was everything for him to know that he was making a worthwhile contribution to his community.

The looks on the faces of the people who blessed the Jewish community were imprinted on his mind. Now more of the JIAS hard work began to bear fruit. After much pressuring from JIAS, the Canadian Government saw to it that no emigrants were permitted to sail from Europe to Canada unless they complied with all the regulations. This prevented the heartbreak of those who arrived here with every hope of starting a new life only to be jailed and then shipped back to Europe.

During the summer of 1922, the Government implemented more stringent regulations, practically prohibiting entry into the country to Jews from Eastern Europe. Only wives destined to their husbands, minor children joining their parents, and farmers, farm labourers, or domestics (provided they had reasonable assurance of employment) were admitted. Fewer immigrants arrived and the JIAS staff was reduced. The headquarters moved to smaller offices on St. Lawrence Boulevard at the corner of Sherbrooke Street.

Then in the fall of 1923 an event took place that demanded rescue of epic proportions. Five thousand Ukrainian Jews, having escaped the pogroms in their own country, were stranded in Romania. The Romanian government had ordered them to leave or else be sent back to the Ukraine. No country was willing to take them in. The Jewish Colonization Association appealed to Ottawa on their behalf. Fortunately, The Honourable Mr. Robb, Minister of Immigration, was sympathetic to this urgent cause and granted a concession for the entry of the 5,000 refugees at the rate of 100 a week, with the understanding that the J.C.A. would be responsible for them.

The immense operation of receiving these immigrants, distributing and placing them throughout the country, (40% to be retained in Montreal and the East, 30% in Ontario, and 30% in Western Canada) and caring for them until they were finally integrated was of such magnitude that only those closely in touch with the Society could appreciate all the work that was being done. JIAS branches in Toronto, Winnipeg, London, Fort William, Regina, Saskatoon, Calgary, Edmonton, Vancouver were completely reorganized, and new branches were established elsewhere in order to handle the enormity of the task at hand.

The Jewish community was involved in every aspect of the project. Butchers contributed meat, bakers gave bread; manufacturers and wholesalers donated clothing and furniture. Financial contributions came not only from Canadians, but also from New York and from J.C.A. in Paris.

Finally, in mid-November 1924, the last group arrived. Bernard, accompanied by Lyon Cohen, a leading member of the Jewish community, travelled to Halifax where they were joined by S. B. Kaufman of the Emergency Jewish Immigration Committee, Toronto. They were to meet the immigrants who arrived on the *President Wilson*. The boat arrived in quarantine on November 19th, late in the afternoon, and the immigrants were not able to land before the next morning. Permission from the immigration authorities was granted to the three men to board ship in the evening to register the immigrants and to commence the work of distributing them throughout the country. They spent all night working on the boat, and the work continued into the following day. When the immigrants landed in the morning, 60 of them were detained after the first medical examination. Work had to continue to facilitate the release of the immigrants detained. There was a second and then a third examination until, with steady intervention, all were finally released at the end of the day.

Now Bernard and the two other men had to ensure that the immigrants destined to the West travelled by direct route from Quebec to Winnipeg for their own safety. In the past many immigrants had escaped from the trains and disappeared into the cities of Montreal and Toronto, which rendered them liable to detention and deportation. Lyon Cohen took charge of the 187 immigrants destined to the West from Halifax on the Maritime Express until they reached Quebec, when they were handed over to a representative of the JIAS Winnipeg branch. Bernard and S.B. Kaufman took charge of the Montreal and Toronto groups travelling by special train from Halifax to Montreal and Toronto.

When the last 100 of 3400 refugees had been admitted into Canada, the Canadian Government closed its doors to further immigrants. The Immigration Department stated that the agreement had been restricted specifically to Russian Jews stranded in Romania. Others not fitting that description were inadmissible.

This humanitarian cause of such immense proportions - a matter of life and death to thousands of human beings - had from the beginning energized and motivated Bernard to, as he said, "move mountains" to assist. Remembering his own personal obstacles, his struggle in the new world, his ambition and drive, he had summoned that indefatigable energy, commitment and dedication to help others whose needs were even greater than his had been.

Bernard was still unable to abandon his dream of graduate work and eventually becoming an academic. He allowed himself a year to settle into the post at JIAS and then added to his horrendous workload further studies for his M.A. degree. Queen's University, his alma mater, had accepted him as a correspondence Masters candidate. By 1923 he had completed the five required

courses, and submitted his thesis topic, "Jewish Immigration in Canada," that would tie in with his work at JIAS However, the demands of his work - the meetings, the preparing of briefs, the travelling - coupled with the obligations of fulfilling the duties of a loving husband, precluded the completion of the thesis. Reluctantly he gave it up. The Masters degree was not in the cards at this time.

ABE FRIEDGUT

Meanwhile, Abe Friedgut and Bernard kept in close touch. Abe, having no marital responsibilities, had entered University of Manitoba to pursue a law degree. Bernard followed Abe's progress and was proud of his decision to study law. In 1924, when Abe graduated, he returned to Regina where he set up a law practice and the following year he married his sweetheart, Judith.

While Bernard was occupied with his post at JIAS, his own sweetheart, Dora, continued with her activities except that, like most women of her generation, once married, she never worked again. Instead she concentrated on vocal and piano studies. One of the first items they had bought for their new home was a Willis piano. What was a house without a piano? She could not conceive of such a thing.

There was an additional way to enhance their enjoyment of music at home, to be able to hear the greatest voices and symphony conductors right in their own parlour! It would entail buying a Victrola. Bernard was earning a good living now and they could afford it. They set out to shop for one. Archambault on Ste. Catherine Street had the best selection where they found a Gerhard Heintzman Phonograph "guaranteed to produce the highest quality tone." Contained in a mahogany cabinet, it was a handsome piece of furniture.

Gradually the couple accumulated an impressive record collection. Records were expensive, costing from $.90 to $1.65 each. Nevertheless they were worth it. Before long they had in their possession well over 100 records. Their taste was eclectic, consisting of operatic music - their favourite - and music by Shubert, Chopin, Liszt, Rimsky Korsakow, and Moussorgsky. Also in their collection were popular songs, dance music to practice by - foxtrots such as "Linger Awhile" and "I'm Singing Pretty in a Pretty Little City" with the California Ramblers, waltzes such as "Memory Lane" with the Romancers, and music in a variety of languages - Russian, Hebrew, Yiddish, and German. A proud acquisition was a recording of Enrico Caruso, the first opera star to be recorded, singing excerpts from *Aida*.

Meanwhile Dora's sister Rachel had become the star of the family. Today she would have been called a feminist. Her ambition had been to be a dentist, but females in Quebec were not permitted to enter the dentistry field. Determined to be involved in the profession, she left Montreal to attend the School of Mechanical Dentistry in New York. As part of her training she apprenticed with a New York dentist.

Armed with her credentials, she returned to Montreal and managed to obtain a position as a dental assistant, becoming the first woman in that profession in Montreal and possibly the whole of Canada. Rachel confided to Dora that from time to time her boss discreetly allowed her to do fillings and other dental work.

Gradually, as more women were hired in her field, Rachel announced to her family that it was time to elevate the status of dental assistants not only for herself but also for her female peers. How would she accomplish this? With door-to-door involvement. Dora and her sisters listened in awe as Rachel described to them how she personally marched into dentists' offices and removed mops from assistants' hands. She insisted that patients book appointments, not the current practice of the day. In 1926 she brought together a small group of French, English and Jewish female dental assistants to form The Montreal Dental Assistants Association (MDAA).

Dora, her sister, led a more typical married life. However, Bernard often needed to travel to Ottawa to attend meetings, or to Winnipeg or Halifax to greet new immigrants. Dora, used to being in a household of ten, was uneasy spending nights alone. When she married her parents had emphasized that her room would remain untouched in case she ever needed access to it. On those lonely nights when Bernard was away, she would stay with her parents and siblings in the house in which she grew up. Not a day would pass, however, without receiving a loving postcard from her husband.

DAVID HALTRECHT

> To My Dear Wife
> This is the message I want to convey to you.
> You're just as dear
> And my love is true
> Tho' I am miles
> Away from you.

While Dora and Bernard were enjoying this comfortable lifestyle, Bernard's brother, David, was still in Berlin with his family. Notwithstanding that their affluent social and cultural existence was more or less intact, David was growing increasingly concerned about the political climate in Germany and he thought he should test the waters in Palestine. So in 1924, together with his wife and their daughter, he embarked on what they hoped would be a new life in a welcoming country. His sister and her husband had settled there, and that was an added incentive for him. The three sons, in their 20s, remained in Berlin.

David, a successful tobacco merchant, looked around to see what type of business might succeed in his new environment. And he hit upon an idea - to build and operate an open-air movie theatre. But the business failed and, after a year or so, he felt forced to look elsewhere. In the meantime Bernard had been trying to persuade his brother to emigrate to Montreal where he could try, once again, to establish a future home for his family. At last David agreed. This time, however, he would not uproot the others. Once established, he would send for them.

Bernard, of course, was thrilled to have his only brother near him. When they had last seen each other Bernard was just a youngster away from home for the first time. David worked tirelessly, placing all his energies into establishing a tobacco business that he named Oriental Tobacco. He was putting in long hours seven days a week, and was consumed with anxiety about being able to build a successful enough enterprise to maintain the standards at which he had supported his family in Berlin.

David's fatigue and anxieties were of serious concern to Bernard. This unfair situation could not continue. It was time David's offspring, no longer children, assumed some financial responsibilities in their lives. There they were in Berlin, squandering their time in leisurely activities, while their father was struggling to earn a living in a new country. Bernard decided to take matters into his own hands. He would write to his nephews and advise them of the directions they should take.

48 St. Louis Square
Montreal, Que.
August 30, 1926

"My dear nephews, Moritz, Arnold and Albert,

You may be surprised to hear from me so suddenly but it is the unexpected thrills that make a person's life interesting. I am moved to write you this letter by the present unusual circumstances of your broken-up family life, when one-sixth of your family is in Montreal, one-third in Palestine, and half in Berlin. I therefore hope that you will give this letter the serious thought in which it is written, and examine closely the remarks and suggestions that it contains.

I need hardly tell you how happy we all were to see your father David come here. This remark applies particularly to me personally. Your father is my only brother, whom I had not seen for 17 years, and his life and happiness are as dear to me as my own. At the same time I must say, I am filled with consternation to observe that you, three young sons in full bloom, instead of endeavouring to establish a home for your mother and father in their approaching old age, instead of telling your parents that they have done enough for you when they had the means, and now it is your duty to reciprocate, you allow your aged, worn out father to go into the world and to begin a new struggle for existence.

You expect him to prepare the foundation for you in the New World, while you remain in Germany - your native but inhospitable country - wasting away your young and best years. Is this fair? Is this right?

I left my home in Poland when I was only 13, and when I reached Canada, a strange country - I knew nobody and nobody knew me - I was 19 years of age. It is true I had to struggle for some time, but this struggle made me what I am today. It is the struggle for existence that makes life worth living. It is the struggle for existence that is the cause of all progress and the mainstay of our civilization.

You, Moritz, being the eldest of the three, must show an example to your younger brothers. You must be daring and courageous. You should go to New York. Millions of young men and women have gone to the United States of America during the past fifty years and have succeeded. It is up to you to do the same thing.

The German quota to the United States is large, and being born in Germany you are entitled to be passed on the German quota in the same way as Henry and Moritz Pipersberg [their cousins, children of Selma Haltrecht Pipersberg]. There are rumours that next year the United States will reduce the immigration quotas from all countries, and therefore if you wait you may be too late.

Next Arnold. Your place is Montreal. No one appreciates studies better than I do. But having a trade in hand, and with your knowledge of music you may be able to find an existence here. With you in Montreal and Moritz in New York, you will see which is the better and more practical place to establish a home.

You, Albert, the youngest of the three, should for the time being remain in Berlin to look after your mother and sister until such a time when a home is prepared for them on this side. You have a position, and are therefore able to take care of them, temporarily, at least.

You must think and act at once. Your father feels broken-hearted at the thought that you do not even appear to dream about settling down. He has given his years, his health, his very life for you. No matter what you will do, you cannot repay the debt you owe him. Try at least to do your duty in a small way. I feel fully convinced that my words will not fall on deaf ears.

I am writing this letter without your father's knowledge. So please do not mention one word about it when you write to him. It would hurt him very much to know that I have written you such a letter. At the same time I feel that it is nothing but right that you should be fully acquainted with the situation. I have not the slightest doubt that you will answer me soon. You can send your reply in German, in case English is too difficult for you.

With kindest regards and love to the three of you, I am

Your uncle

Sally alias Bernard

MORITZ, ARNOLD, ALBERT - BERLIN

Bernard's warnings proved to be correct. Not long after, immigration quotas were substantially reduced. By 1929, Jews had virtually been barred from Canada. The nephews took their uncle's advice and the whole family emigrated from Germany the following year. Having money and connections smoothed the way through the bureaucracy.

The move to North America not only removed the family from a hostile environment, but also permitted remarkable education, particularly for Arnold, one of David's children, who later studied at Princeton University where he had occasion to meet the illustrious professor, Albert Einstein. In their walks on campus, they discovered that they both played the violin, though neither could envision earning their living from that particular talent. Arnold became an electrical engineer and moved to Ottawa, Ontario, where, recognized as an accomplished violinist, he was invited to become a member of the Ottawa Symphony, with whom he performed for many years.

Arnold's sister, Margot, was a contralto who was devoted to her singing. Although she never pursued singing as a career, she sang publicly all her life. No wedding or other family function would have been complete without a rendition by Margot. She would even sing at her own funeral! In preparation for her death, she recorded a dirge with instructions that it be played at her funeral.

Years later, Earl, Albert's youngest son, would read the letter Bernard had sent to his father and uncles, and it would send shivers down his spine. "This letter," he said, "may have saved my father and his family from the Holocaust!"

Bernard did not stop with his brother's family. He also succeeded in persuading three of his sister Masha's children and two of his Haltrecht cousins to emigrate. Bernard now had two of his sisters and their families with him in Montreal. Anna and her husband had emigrated from London, England, and Selma had emigrated with her husband and their four children from Hambourg, Germany. Being surrounded by extended family was heartwarming. Although he had been embraced first by the Ratner family, then in his days out West by the Friedgut family, Bernard was overjoyed to have his blood relations near him. The youngest of his siblings, he became the patriarch of the family. The family members would come to him for advice, support, and solace during difficult times, and, at their invitation, he would hold centre stage during many of the family celebrations.

In 1927, the year that David's family emigrated to Montreal, Bernard was offered the position of supervising-editor-in-charge of a proposed new Jewish Daily. He was offered a five-year contract at $5,000 a year. Committed to his work with JIAS, he turned it down. Had he suspected that his position would soon become obsolete with the end of Jewish immigration to Canada, he still would not have deserted his post prematurely.

Despite all the exhaustive efforts of the Canadian Jewish Congress, JIAS, and the Jewish community in general, that is exactly what happened. Two years later, in 1929, Jewish immigrants were no longer permitted to come into Canada. On a national and international level, the new policy was a disaster. On a personal level, for Bernard, the challenging, meaningful, stimulating work was over.

For many months the image of those Eastern European Jews denied access to Canada haunted him. Try as he might, he could not help envisioning the horrific fate that awaited them. Imprinted in his memory, too, were thousands of Montreal faces. These were the people who had appeared in his office over the years crying and begging him to help save their relatives and friends. There was a myriad of stories, a myriad of difficulties. Sometimes Bernard could help, sometimes he could not. But he always made a supreme effort in an unassuming manner. Such was his personality.

Those who had been fortunate enough to arrive safely had often rushed to kiss the ground the minute they disembarked. Yes, success could be gratifying, even euphoric, and failure was bitterly disappointing. After all the heroic effort, some immigrants were sent back later and Bernard suffered with them their horror and disappointment. And there were always more Jews waiting anxiously in Europe to be brought over.

Now, after years of doing something so important with his life, he was suddenly cut off. Bernard was resilient, he knew he would move on, but his sense of loss was keen. On the last day in his office, well-wishers crowded in to offer appreciation and personal thank-yous, but as he packed up his last papers and books, shut the door to his office, and walked down the familiar corridor for the last time, there was a sense of disheartening finality and sadness.

15 ✡ PARENTHOOD

Aside from having serious worries and fears for his compatriots in Europe, Bernard was without a job. It would not be easy to acquire another one now. There was a depression and unemployment was rampant. He would have to be a self-starter. On one of his trips to New York he had met Dr. C. Jaeger, a scientist, who had a laboratory in New York. Dr. Jaeger had developed a liquid called Gerbaulin Belt Food that prolonged the life of automobile belts. The product had so far not been manufactured in Canada. Bernard, convinced that this would be a viable product for Canada, formed a company called "Haltjaeg Products." Running a plant of this nature involved salesmanship which necessitated travel. It was a way to make a living, but this type of work was an unsatisfactory occupation for his intellectual disposition. To add to the disappointment in Bernard's professional life, two deaths occurred, one on each side of the family. On November 6, 1929, the patriarch of Dora's family, Samuel David Uriah Ratner, died. His demise was a sad blow to Dora, who had felt

close to her father. Samuel's death was followed six months later by that of Bernard's brother, David, who died unexpectedly while undergoing minor surgery.

The bright spot in Dora and Bernard's life occurred that same year when they learned that Dora was pregnant. What a thrill! Nine years of marriage and no conception had occurred. They had given up hope of ever having children, and then, out of the blue, a child was expected. When Dora announced to her siblings that she was pregnant, they were sceptical. Up until now neither Dora nor Rebecca, who had married Henry Green a few years earlier, had conceived a child. They were convinced their sister was fantasizing and the alleged baby was nothing more than a tumour.

REBECCA AND HENRY

During Dora's pregnancy she made sure to visit art galleries to view beautiful paintings, to attend concerts and generally ensure that her unborn child would be exposed to pleasant, relaxing experiences.

Stanley David, named after his late maternal grandfather, was born March 25th, 1931, at 4:43 a.m. at the Royal Victoria Hospital. It was a long labour, but when Dora set eyes upon her son, she thought of her father and how he would have cherished having a grandson. Now Bernard had a son to whom he could hand down the Haltrecht name. On April 6th, the baby was taken to his parents' home at 258 St. Louis Square.

The news spread fast and gifts poured in from family and friends. Annie immediately brought over a baby book so that a record could be kept of the baby's progress. The proud new father willingly assumed the task of recording every detail of his son's growth and accomplishments. Gradually the book became filled, not only with hand-written notes, but also with photographs of the baby - alone, with his parents, with his aunts and uncles and with his grandmother.

Bernard wanted to make sure that his son would be advised of his roots and the heritage of his surname. So he inscribed the family history into Stanley's baby book:

"The name 'Haltrecht,' meaning 'keep right,' originated in the latter part of the 18th Century in Poland. Our ancestor Noah Haltrecht was first given that name in the form of a nickname, because he was a famous judge in Rabbinical Law. He was one of the main founders of the religious Renaissance raging in the 18th century among Russian and Polish Jewry. Among his famous works of the time was his *Toldas Noah* meaning 'The Generations of Noah,' which also became his pen name. Until recent years his sermons were studied by the various Rabbinates of Eastern European Jewry. On his death a day of mourning was set aside by Russian and Polish Jewry. Arnold Haltrecht still has some original manuscripts in his possession. The Renaissance movement of which Noah was such an integral part is known as *Misnagdismus.*"

A new phase in the lives of Dora and Bernard had begun. Now they lived, not only for each other, but also for their son. After the ritual circumcision, it was time to plan for the "First Born" ceremony. According to custom, thirty days following Stanley's birth, a *Pidyon Haben* ritual (Redemption of the First Born) took place in their home. Baby Stanley was dressed in his best clothes. Dora and the nurse placed him on a silver tray, while the guests decorated him with jewels of all sorts. Bernard held his son on the tray while jointly performing the ceremony with the "Priest." And what was that ceremony? Bernard was required to "buy" his boy from the Priest for a specified sum. Traditionally, the firstborn of Israel were supposed to be dedicated to God (Exodus 13:1-2) and were expected to perform religious services for the priests (*Kohanim*). According to the biblical command, they could be redeemed, that is, bought back from God by their parents with five shekels. This redemption is the purpose of *Pidyon Haben.*

When it was announced there was to be an eclipse of the sun on August 31st of that year, they wanted to make sure that the five-month old infant did not miss this historic event. At the appointed moment, Dora dressed Stanley and took the infant onto the balcony to witness the astronomical spectacle. Due to clouds in the sky, however, very little could be seen, except total darkness for about half a minute, and partial darkness for over two hours. Still, it was a moment in history to be recorded in the "book."

After ten years of awaiting a first child, they did not expect a second child. But two years later a baby girl followed. A millionaire's family!, said Bernard. Theirs were the only offspring produced from the Ratner family of eight children. None of Dora's siblings had married except Rebecca, who was childless.

STANLEY

119

Stanley had been named for his maternal grandfather, Samuel David. Now it was Bernard's family's turn. The new baby was named Muriel Nora after her paternal grandmother and grandfather - Muriel for Mary and Nora for Noah. A pink silk baby book, similar to Stanley's blue one, was purchased and her progress and accomplishments began to be recorded. Since this was a female child, there were no rituals required.

This child proved to be a tomboy. Being the athlete in the family, she liked climbing and tumbling and was very active. She adored her big brother. When her hair began to grow in, forming white curls, her aunts nicknamed her "snowball."

STANLEY AND MURIEL

The Ratner family delighted in living across the street from Dora and Bernard where they could visit with them daily and see the children. They loved to wheel them in their carriages in St. Louis Square. But even though it was clearly an advantage for the two families to live in such close proximity, Dora and Bernard were growing dissatisfied with the neighbourhood. There was a depression and poverty was evident in central Montreal. Ancient buildings were becoming dilapidated and they were finding the atmosphere somewhat dismal.

They were also planning ahead for their children's schooling. The trend was to move westward and they had heard that the Outremont schools had an excellent reputation. They began to plant the seed in the family's mind that they were thinking along these lines and the siblings were supportive. They were already trying to convince their mother to move.

Dora and Bernard found a very pleasant duplex on Davaar Avenue near Lajoie in Outremont. It had a lovely sunroom and a back yard where the children would be able to play safely. Moreover, it was situated within short walking distance of two beautiful parks. Joyce Park was the smaller of the two. Its tranquil setting and its well-manicured landscape were most appealing. Pratt Park was larger and offered more activities, such as skating and tobogganing in the winter, which would serve the children well as they grew older.

As things turned out, they were not to live there very long. Over the years Bernard and Dora had accumulated savings and had invested some of the money in some properties. On one of these properties, a house in Notre Dame de Grace, they held a second mortgage. In these tough times, the residents of the house could no longer afford the payments. Therefore Dora and Bernard left Outremont to live as homeowners.

Thrilled as he was with his expanded family and his newly acquired residence, Bernard was not at all thrilled with the way his professional life had stagnated.

What had happened to all his dreams? An academic life and a fulfilling career were all gone by the wayside. He talked it over with Dora. As he spoke, she could see in his eyes the Bernard of their youth - the ambition, the determination, the dreams. How could she deny him this attempt to reinstate himself academically? It would mean sacrifices, but they had savings and they would have to manage.

In 1935, at age 43, with a wife and two young children to support, Bernard decided to resume his studies. For a man with a family, the best solution would be to prepare for a career in which he could establish his own practice and not be dependent on others. In the past he had been interested in the law profession. In fact, some years earlier he had written to universities to investigate possibilities to study law "off campus" by correspondence while he was otherwise engaged in earning a living. He had been informed that this course of study was not available. The only way he could accomplish this aim was to return to university full time. He wondered whether the confrontational aspect of law would suit his temperament. However, in Quebec, unlike the other provinces in Canada, a legal profession had been established to deal exclusively with non-contentious matters.

He applied to the law department at McGill with the view of becoming a notary. The Dean of Law was polite but discouraged him. He was too old, he had a family to support; he cited examples of men Bernard's age who had tried to re-enter university and failed. He did not specifically mention the quota of Jewish students allowed into McGill. In any case, Bernard was aware of this further obstacle. Undaunted, he persisted and was eventually accepted.

In the fall of 1936 he began to attend classes. He indentured in a notarial office during the day, continued with his Haltjaeg business commitments, and studied into the wee hours of the night. While his fellow students enjoyed camaraderie on campus, he himself did not have a chance to even find the library until exam time in December. Nevertheless, he passed that first year ranking third in his class. He had cleared the first hurdle. An unexpected hurdle followed fast.

16 ✡ THE LAWSUIT

In May, 1937, the Board of Notaries decided that in spite of the fact that Bernard had done so well academically, they could not permit him to continue his studies because he had not produced a satisfactory birth certificate. Thus began a litany of reasons for him not to be accepted by the Board. That summer was a horrendous experience.

Having submitted numerous documents which Mr. Courtois, the secretary, kept requesting, such as his naturalization papers, his identification papers, and diploma and transcript from Queen's, Bernard became suspicious of Mr. Courtois' intentions when he was asked for further documents of identification.

However, he politely inquired as to what further documents the secretary would like him to produce. Trying to be helpful, Bernard told him that he had an official graduation year book where Mr. Courtois could find both his photograph as well as a brief biography. Bernard then suggested that a number of prominent men in the city of Montreal could identify him in person. "No," said Mr. Courtois. "That would not be sufficient." Then, looking over the certificate of studies in Bernard's file, he said, "I don't see any philosophy." Bernard walked over to his chair and pointed to a course in Mental Philosophy. Mr. Courtois said, "That's right," and apologized for overlooking it. Finally he asked, "Do you have your birth certificate?"

Bernard was taken aback. He could not believe his ears. Like a schoolmaster to a student, he explained to Mr. Courtois his circumstances. He said, "Mr. Courtois, I was born in Poland. I left it as a small boy, when it was part of the old Russian Empire. Since then that country has undergone a world war, a civil war and a revolution. I heard that during the wars and revolution fighting took place in the streets of the very town where I was born. I am therefore not at all sure whether my records are still in existence. If they are, I could get them. It is a question of time." "Your documents," Mr. Courtois said, "will have to be complete in my hands 15 days prior to the meeting of the Board, namely by June 28."

Bernard was now racing against time to procure the required certificate, if such a certificate existed at all. He immediately proceeded to the office of the Polish consulate on Stanley Street. He told the secretary that he needed a birth certificate from his country. The secretary told him that he had come to the wrong place. He was a British subject, and therefore would have to apply to the British authorities. He advised Bernard to write to the British Consulate in Warsaw, where in turn they would write to the town council of Plock. In due time, he said, Bernard should receive the certificate.

Bernard explained to the secretary that this would be too slow a process, and requested that the secretary communicate by cable directly with the Plock town hall. If his records were there, a birth certificate could be dispatched by air-mail, and he could possibly have it within two weeks. The secretary excused himself, entering the private office of Mr. Wladyslaw Kicki, the Consul, and in a few minutes returned. "I am sorry, Mr. Haltrecht, but Mr. Kicki has asked me to inform you that since you are not a Polish citizen, you are not under our jurisdiction."

But Bernard was not to be turned away. He demanded to see the Consul in person. Seeing the determination on Bernard's face, the secretary reluctantly showed him into the private office. Bernard explained that whereas he realized he had no claim on Polish authorities, this was a very urgent personal matter, and asked him to please send a cable as a special favour. Mr. Kicki said, "A cable to Poland, a cabled reply air mail, birth certificate, consular fees; it is going to cost you a lot of money." "True," Bernard said, "I can ill afford this expense.

But I must have the certificate at all costs. If it arrived a little late, I would at least have the official cable from your government, which I hope will satisfy the Board of Notaries."

On the afternoon of Monday, June 14th, Bernard received a telephone call from the Polish Consulate. They had received a cable. Miraculously the records had been located, and his birth certificate was on its way. Two days later he presented both cables to Mr. Courtois, who looked them over and was satisfied. Bernard was now at liberty to make the official application for the admission to study. It seemed that the matter was now closed. Bernard could breathe a little more easily. But there seemed to be no end to this nightmare.

Two weeks later Bernard received a telegram. It was from Mr. Courtois in Quebec. He was advising Bernard that the Board had rejected his application due to lack of a required philosophy course. He said that if Bernard desired to present any arguments he could come to Quebec, since the Board would be in session Wednesday and Thursday. This telegram was a bitter blow.

During Bernard's post at JIAS, he had had dealings with Peter Bercovitch, a prominent Montreal lawyer and Liberal MNA who, a year before, had been selected to defuse a scandal which involved the Liberal party's public spending. Prominent as he was, he himself was the target of anti-Semitism, particularly by Paul Anger in *Le Devoir*. He called on the lawyer now and showed him the telegram. Mr. Bercovitch advised Bernard to go to Quebec. Bernard consequently wired Mr. Courtois that he was coming.

Midnight found him on the train to Quebec. The meeting of the Board of Notaries would be held at the Court House the next morning. He wanted to be alert and prepared for their questions. Although Bernard generally was able to catch a few winks at the drop of a hat, this night was different. His mind was overactive. How had he arrived in this situation? Why were there so many obstacles? He resolved to handle this obstacle in his usual persistent manner. It was a temporary stumbling block. The Board had to decide in his favour.

It was important for him to succeed, not only for himself, but especially for Dora and the children. They deserved to have an easier life than he had known. Certainly, he would not want his son to suffer the hardships that he had had to endure to establish himself in life. Dora had stood by him these past years in his struggles. He needed to prove to her and to himself that he could accomplish his goal. He knew that she supported him in his struggles to earn his law degree to become a notary.

It could not have been easy for her to go along with him in his decision to return to university at his age against so many odds, with a family to support, and in light of the quota of Jewish students at McGill. To her credit, she never discouraged him. Nor, he felt, did she encourage him. Never mind, he had enough determination for both of them. This latest obstacle, one they had not foreseen, was placed in his path by the largely francophone Board of Notaries, which was trying to prevent him from continuing his studies.

The train arrived. Bernard found his way to the courthouse. He would never forget this day, a day which stretched into late evening as he sat on a hard wooden bench outside the Board room waiting and waiting for the decision that would decide his future. The decision came at 11:30 p.m. His appeal had been rejected.

The Board decreed that in 1921 (some 18 years before) when he had graduated from Queen's, Bernard had not taken a certain philosophy course that the Board now decided was a pre-requisite for notaries. This affront was the last straw. (It is noteworthy that the two other students who were refused acceptance by the Board were Jewish graduates from English-language universities.) Determined to succeed, Bernard hired lawyer Peter Bercovitch, thereby becoming the first student in history to sue the Board of Notaries. On the appointed day, July 27, 1937, they appeared in Court.

The decision that would be handed down would seal Bernard's fate. He knew he had "right" on his side and he had faith in the judicial system. The Honourable Mr. Judge Fortier listened carefully to the arguments on both sides after which he rendered the following decision.

PROVINCE OF QUEBEC   S U P E R I O R   C O U R T
DISTRICT OF MONTREAL
NO. 167151
ON THIS 27TH day of July 1937
P R E S E N T:
THE HON: MR. JUSTICE FORTIER

SALEK BERNARD HALTRECHT, Law Student
of the city of Montreal,
Petitioner
vs.
THE BOARD OF NOTARIES, of the Province
of Quebec, a body politic and corporate,
having its corporate seat in the city of
Montreal,
Respondent

THE COURT, having heard the parties by counsel on Petitioner's petition praying, for the reasons therein set forth duly of article 992 et. seq. C.P., ordering the Respondents to appear before the Court to answer the demand contained in the said petition and to show cause why they should refuse to

register the Petitioner as a duly qualified notarial student of the Province of
Quebec;

DOTH GRANT the said petition as prayed; let the said writ issue; costs to
follow.

sig. H.-A. Fortier
J.S.C.M.
JOM/TG

They won the case! Bernard could continue his studies! In the depths of
his heart he had known he would succeed. Like a resolute athlete centred on a
single goal, his entire entity had been focused on winning. He had done everything
in his power, called upon all his energies and resources to overcome the intolerance
and unjust prejudice of those in power. It was more than one student's fight to
continue his education; there was an altruistic aspect to the affair. It was a fight
for justice, for human rights. The winning of this case could set a precedent for
students who encountered similar roadblocks in the future.

Bernard was a man who had considered himself "assimilated," not in the
sense of disowning his Jewish identity, but in the sense that he had always
maintained friendships with Gentiles and Jews alike. This was true of his
friendships in London, in Saskatchewan, and in Kingston at Queen's. He was a
man who was appalled by social injustice and discrimination. He dreamed of
solidarity among all religions and faiths. It was an attitude of tolerance and
acceptance that he advocated to others and one which he would pass on to his
children.

He realized that in the scheme of things his own personal sacrifices were
nothing compared to what his fellow Jews had suffered in their countries of
origin. The persecution he had undergone was a personal case; moreover, it was
not life threatening, either for him or for his family. Nevertheless he found it
symbolic of the ethnic prejudice that crept into countries and infected its people.
It was insidious in its subtlety. In this case, being rejected by the very men he had
hoped would become his colleagues was especially troublesome and even painful.

He was now vindicated. And he would move on.

In 1939 Bernard graduated from law school. He obtained a B.C.L. (Bachelor
of Civil Law), passed the Board of Notary exams and finally reached his goal.
He hung out his shingle. The struggle was over. He had a profession now to
hand down to his son.

III

THE NEXT GENERATION:
STANLEY AND MURIEL

17 ✿ OUTREMONT, NDG, AND BACK

My earliest memory is of moving from our rented duplex on Davaar Avenue near Lajoie in Outremont to our own home, an eight-room two-storey house on Hingston Avenue in Notre Dame de Grace in late spring, 1936. Two muscular men removed every piece of furniture from our house and placed it into a big red truck. Mother, looking flushed and excited, brought Stanley and me into the sunroom and fed us egg and salmon sandwiches instead of our customary full-course lunch. My father, with his typical energy, supervised and also rushed back and forth helping the movers.

When the house had been completely emptied, the four of us climbed into my father's black Chevrolet and followed the truck to our new house. It was a happy event.

Two years later, when Father was struggling to make ends meet while studying in law school, tragedy befell both sides of the family. My mother's sister, Rachel, the "star" of the Ratner family, died of cancer in February at the age of 45, and my grandmother, Chvolas, died in May of the following year. My only recollection of aunt Rachel was that in the last days of her life, she called me into her bedroom in NDG, removed a ring from her little finger, and placed it on my middle finger. It was silver, heart-shaped and had her initials on it, R.R.

Aunt Annie, witnessing this ceremony, burst into tears and rushed out of the room, but mother pulled me aside. When I asked why auntie was crying, she tried to make light of the situation, distracting me by re-arranging my curls and re-tying the pink ribbon in my hair, but I could see that she, too, had tears in her eyes. In retrospect, Mother was unable to tell me the truth because, in her opinion, illness and death were not topics for her children's ears. Just as her parents had shielded her from the ugliness surrounding their lives in Russia, she wished us to enjoy our childhood free from tragedy. Besides, she was uncomfortable around such a display of emotion.

I loved my aunt Rachel's ring and wore it every day. Later, the children at school would always ask what the initials stood for. When I would tell them they were the initials of my aunt who had died, they would listen most solemnly.

On a chilly February day hundreds of mourners congregated in the Paperman funeral parlour on St. Urbain Street to pay tribute to Rachel Ratner, their friend and colleague. It was unusual to see so many Christians at a Jewish funeral, but Rachel had been widely known and respected particularly in the dental community. Most of the Christians in attendance had never before been to a Jewish funeral, and as they listened to the mournful chanting of the cantor, they were caught up in the shared grief. At the time I was unaware of aunt Rachel's stature and accomplishments, but her colleagues remembered her and spoke eloquently of her.

The Ratners had been members of the *Chevra Kadisha* Synagogue on Cadieux Street near Vitré since their arrival in Montreal, and were well known to the Rabbi and the congregation. This familiarity with the family coupled with the premature death of a respected member of the community was reflected in his eulogy. Fighting back his own tears, the Rabbi recalled personal memories of Rachel and acknowledged her accomplishments and contributions to the greater community. Chvolas, together with her children, Rachel's sisters and brothers, were seated in the mourners' box. They listened intently to the emotional eulogy that echoed their own feelings of sorrow and pride, and did their best throughout the service to maintain their composure.

Adhering to custom, the family mourners, followed by the hundreds in attendance, filed behind the casket out of the funeral parlour onto the street. They passed by the *Stepener* Synagogue, then stopped in front of the *Chevra Shaas* Synagogue, the principal orthodox synagogue in the city, to listen to the cantor chant a special prayer. Meanwhile the hearse, with its dominating wooden top, moved quietly beside the mourners. A number of sleek black limousines stayed close behind the hearse waiting to drive passengers to the *Chevra Kadisha* cemetery on Sauvé Street. In his role as funeral director, Mr. Paperman, in morning coat, striped pants, and derby hat, was discreetly on hand to supervise the procedure.

Papermans was in an entirely Jewish area and news travelled fast. Those who were not in attendance at the actual service watched the crowds coming and going from behind their curtained windows. But their children were pulled away from the windows because Jewish children were not permitted to attend or watch funeral processions. It was considered bad luck.

Afterwards, on the steps of the funeral parlour, members of the Montreal Dental Assistants Association shared reflections of Rachel's accomplishments. The president, Margaret Good, reminded the others that Rachel was the first dental assistant in Montreal and possibly in all of Canada. "Let us not forget that she paved the way for all of us in the profession to gain the respect of dentists, respect that we now sometimes take for granted," she said.

At their annual provincial meetings, conventions and banquets across the country, memorial services were held for Rachel. Speaker after speaker talked of the loss to the association of their inspirational and dynamic founder. The letters of condolence that were sent to the Ratner family, advising them of these services, provided considerable comfort.

Two years later when Quebec women gained the vote, Rachel's colleagues regretted that Rachel was not with them to share this moment of joy and accomplishment. Every year following her death they would commemorate her at their Annual Founders Dinner by giving a brief description of her background, describing her

RACHEL RATNER

128

struggles and determination to elevate the status of the mechanical dentistry profession, and pointing out her personal qualities.

In May, 1938, three months after Rachel's death, Father's sister, Selma, and her husband, Adolf Pipersberg, lost their 24-year old daughter, Margo, to tuberculosis. Nine weeks later Adolf died. Aunt Selma, left on her own, came to live with us in NDG, where there was ample room for her. She brought some belongings, one of which was a magnificent grandfather's clock that would adorn our foyer. An accomplished seamstress, her foot-treadle sewing machine would often be heard clicking away upstairs in her room, and this hobby helped her retain her sanity under the tragic circumstances of four family deaths in more than one year.

Our parents' losses of immediate family were heartfelt, but the news filtering in from Germany was horrifying. Jews were being stripped of their rights, expelled from their own country, and sent to concentration camps.

AUNT SELMA

In December 1939, after the Allies had declared war, Abe Friedgut, my father's dearest friend, enlisted in the army as a second lieutenant and went overseas. Masha, my father's only sibling who did not leave Poland, was eventually rounded up with her husband, Aaron, and remaining children, and sent off to concentration camp. They were never heard from again.

For our parents, Bernard and Dora, their children's childhood was sacrosanct and they would protect it from news of this sort. Discussions on the topic of anti-Semitic atrocities were conducted in whispers in Yiddish, a language with which Stanley and I were unfamiliar. Even when I asked for my maternal grandmother or for Mother's sister, auntie Rae, they said they had gone to California. Since that was where my auntie Becky and uncle Henry lived, I accepted this explanation. In this manner, pre-occupied with my own little world, I was kept blissfully unaware both of the tragic world events, and of my father's personal struggles. My brother, being older, was not so easily deceived.

My brother Stanley and I were the only Jewish kids on our street. In fact, we lived opposite an Anglican church. The minister's house was attached to the church, and his son, Grant, was my "boyfriend." Grant, a few months younger than I, was in kindergarten. Although I wasn't quite six years old, my mother had managed to get me into grade one. Grant got home from school before I did and always waited faithfully for me on our veranda. If it was a nice day, we

STANLEY

would have our milk and chocolate marshmallow biscuits out there, after which we would play.

One day he took me to a church service. When the congregation kneeled I didn't know what I was supposed to do, so after cautiously looking from left to right, I kneeled too. Upon returning home, I reported this quandary to my mother, who responded, "You didn't kneel, did you?" When I answered that I had, she suggested it would be best if I didn't attend any more church services.

Everyone I knew had Christmas trees in their houses and received fabulous gifts. Why didn't we? The answers were never satisfactory. That was before the time Jewish parents compensated their children by placing giant electric menorahs in their windows and making a fuss about *Chanukah*, but I still wonder if any holiday can equal the excitement of Christmas with Santa Claus sliding down the chimney to fill stockings with goodies.

Also my friends all had fish on Fridays while we had chicken. My mother's response to that was that we were the lucky ones. In her estimation a meal of chicken was far superior to one of fish. When I stayed home on the Jewish holidays, my school friends would ask, "Where were you? Why weren't you in school?" To which I replied, "It was a holiday." "It was not," they would sneer.

One sunny afternoon Grant, Stanley and I were standing and talking on the sidewalk in front of Grant's house. Some bigger boys came by and started shoving my brother around and pushing him into the shrubs bordering Grant's front garden. Grant ran inside to tell his father. The usually mild-mannered Anglican minister, Reverend Peterson, came out, sternly reprimanded the boys, and sent them on their way. I was impressed that a person of his stature went out of his way to defend a Jewish child from being harmed. I would never forget it.

Another day the census takers came to our door. They were empowered to ask all kinds of personal questions, such as your religion. (For us that was a very personal question.) When my mother answered, "Jewish," one of the census

MURIEL

130

takers said, "Oh my, I never would have thought that you and your little girl were both Jewish, you are both so blonde and fair skinned." In our minds, that was a compliment - not to look Jewish. In the white collar Anglo-Saxon neighbourhood in which we lived, what could be better than looking Anglo-Saxon?

When a kid on the block accused my brother of "killing Christ," my seven-year-old brother explained it was impossible. "Christ was killed long ago, I wasn't even born then," he said. When Stanley reported the incident to our parents, they were very pleased with his astute response and proudly repeated it to our relatives.

Another time some older kids ganged up on me and tried to push me against the concrete wall of their house. There was one girl my size, so I retaliated by giving her a push, then escaping across the street into my house. Before long, the doorbell rang. Mother answered to discover a delegation of children on our front veranda. They said I had scratched this little girl's arm and held it out as evidence of the assault. In her typical non-confrontational style, Mother calmly examined the arm, then asked if they would wait a moment while she went into the house to get her glasses. She returned wearing glasses, and once again examined the arm. She said she was still unable to see any scratch. The group dispersed. A little later the doorbell rang. Some girls my age asked, a little too innocently, if I would come out to play. I was suspicious, so I stepped out on the veranda and looked over the railing. My hunch was correct because two older boys were hiding under the veranda, waiting, I was sure, to take matters in their own hands. I declined their invitation.

That evening Mother related the entire story to my father. She described how, when threatened by a gang of older kids, her little daughter, the tomboy, was able not only to escape from harm, but was also quick to retaliate. They were quite amused by the incident and proud of their little warrior.

4037 HINGSTON AVENUE

In 1939 my father received his Law degree and passed the Board of Notaries. He proudly hung his shiny brass shingle on the front door of our home at 4037 Hingston Avenue. It read, "S. B. Haltrecht, Notary Public." The excitement in the house was infectious and I sensed this was an important symbol. Also, the kids on the street would crowd around our veranda to ask what it meant. "Notary Public, it's like a lawyer," I responded. That was as much as I could tell them then. Father set up his office in the Bank of Montreal Building at 1206 University Street in the heart of downtown Montreal.

The timing of my father's graduation was serendipitous. Shortly after he graduated, the federal government decreed that men married before a certain date would be exempt from the draft. Notaries were therefore in great demand. In the province of Quebec, couples wishing to remain "separate as to property" required a marriage contract in addition to their marriage license. Notaries were the only professionals empowered to fulfill this function.

Imagine the hysteria! What took place became labelled "the rush of marriages" as the phone rang off the hook. One night while my brother, Stanley, and I were sound asleep, an engaged couple rang our doorbell close to midnight, desperate for their documents before the deadline. My father didn't complain. He received them in his dressing gown and gladly drew up their marriage contract.

To develop a high profile to help build his practice, my father wrote a series of articles in *The Monitor* about marriage, women's rights and ownership of property. The newspaper announced "Marriage in the Province of Quebec."

Mr. Haltrecht, the writer of these articles, is an Honours Graduate of Queen's and McGill Universities, a keen student of social and economic problems, and the winner of the Gowan Scholarship in Economics. As a Notary Public for the Province of Quebec, he is in daily touch with people discussing the marriage laws and problems, and he is thus a most competent person to treat on this subject not only from the academic, but also from the practical point of view. The articles will be: Introduction, Fundamental Principles Underlying our Marriage Laws, Community of Property, Separation as to Property, Of Property Reserved to Married Women, The Marriage Contract.

Because of the interest these articles aroused, Father was invited to follow up the series with a weekly column. Citizens sent in their personal legal questions for him to answer in print. The assortment of questions ran the gamut from inquiries about citizenship and rental leases to abandonment, divorce and even bigamy. There were some men and women who wrote "in private" and requested that their letters not be published. My father did not hesitate to respect their confidentiality and responded by private correspondence.

With this type of visibility, he was therefore in some demand to appear at meetings as a guest speaker. Given his background at JIAS, he had previously been invited to discuss questions of immigration, both historical and current. The requests now shifted to topics pertaining to Quebec law, especially the role of women in the province.

The practice was being built relatively quickly, partly due to my father's reputation from his years at JIAS, and partly because he was one of only a handful of Jewish notaries in Montreal. Still, financial resources were limited because the family savings had been depleted during the three years of law studies at McGill, and the house had been mortgaged. Bernard and Dora were forced to face reality. It would take a few more years to build a solid notarial practice. They could no longer afford to live in their own home and it was relinquished to the first mortgagee. They would have to move to a less affluent neighbourhood in a rented flat. Normally, this would have been a sad moment, but they assured each other it was only temporary. They had confidence that before long, they would be able to save enough money to buy their own home again.

Auntie Selma moved to her married son's home in Outremont, taking with her the grandfather's clock I so admired. Henry's wife, Helen, had just given birth to a baby girl, Barbara, and they were now living in a larger flat. Aunt Selma's role as live-in grandmother (two more grandchildren would follow) helped sustain her for the remainder of her life.

When I told my friend Grant that we were moving, he was incredulous. When I told him we were moving to a place called Outremont, he was

FLAT ON DUCHARME

confused and devastated. "You mean it isn't even in NDG?" he asked. "But it's in Montreal, isn't it?" "No," I repeated as calmly as I could, "It is in Outremont." "We'll never see each other again," he said. "Sure we will," I replied. But his prediction proved to be correct. We did not see each other ever again.

In August, one month before I was to enter grade three, we moved to Outremont where our street housed a mixture of Protestants, Catholics and Jews with a variety of parents and ancestry including Scots, Irish and Eastern Europeans. The elementary school we attended in the fall (Guy Drummond) had many Jewish students. Mother often reminded us of that September day when my brother had come home with tears of gratitude in his eyes because the principal had acknowledged the High Holidays in assembly, wishing all the Jewish students a Happy New Year.

I had Jewish friends for the first time in my young life; however, some of them sometimes tormented me for not being able to speak Yiddish. "You're not really Jewish. You don't even speak it." They had learned the language from their immigrant grandparents whereas I only ever knew my mother's mother who had died when I was five years old.

Unlike my Christian friends in NDG, these new friends all celebrated the same holidays as we did. Although our parents were not particularly religious, Mother adhered to the dietary laws, observed all the holidays and lit the *Shabbot* (Sabbath) candles on Friday evenings. Father was more interested in the family aspects of the holidays, but in any case, it was important for all of us to be together Friday evenings. To encourage this happening, we established a Friday evening club with the following hierarchy: Father was president, mother was vice-president, Stanley was treasurer, and I was secretary.

I remember the format. We would have our typical Friday evening dinner (chicken and chicken soup) and then a bridge table would be brought into the parlour. We would take our seats. First we looked at the minutes of the last meeting, and discussed any family business arising from those minutes. We then discussed current events. Father was fiercely interested in politics and so was my brother, but their viewpoints were dissimilar. Then we played bridge.

There was no television at that time to distract families. The radio never blared indiscriminately; it was turned on specifically to hear particular programs. When my father was at home, he listened to the news every hour on the hour. Stanley and I listened to the kids' programs. I remember "Superman" and "Henry Aldrich" which always began with Henry's mother calling, "Hen-ry-y-y!!!" and his nasal response, "Coming, mother." Stanley took great pleasure in trying to scare me with his favourite program, "Inner Sanctum." It was especially scary when our parents were out. He would turn out the lights and cackle in the dark, "Who knows what evil lurks in the hearts of men? Ha, ha, ha, the Shadow knows." Later on, when my friends and I became more sophisticated we would gather at someone's house and, glued to the radio, we would listen to "Lux Radio Theatre," a dramatic series of romantic stories.

Stanley and I loved to tease our mother about the job she had held in the Canadian Pacific Railway office in the years before she married. We used to sing, deliberately off key, "I've been working on the railway all the live long day / I've been working on the railway just to pass the time away-y." We mimed her wielding the pickaxes and shovels she must have used on the railroad tracks. We killed ourselves laughing.

This teasing was doubly amusing because Mother was delicate and quiet spoken. I never heard her raise her voice even when Stanley and I raced through the house or got into a sibling fist-fight; she would intervene in her quiet way. At mealtime, or bedtime, you might hear other mothers loudly calling out for their children to come home. But the most you ever heard from her, were barely audible singsong cadences, "Stan....ley...... Mur....iel, Stan...ley....Mur....iel." There was no shouting, which was clearly not "refined."

While we were growing up our parents talked about future events in our lives with glowing anticipation. Following his thirteenth birthday my brother would have a *Bar Mitzvah*, I would have a Sweet Sixteen, and eventually we would marry and have formal weddings.

It was understood that a Jewish boy studied Hebrew to prepare for his *Bar Mitzvah*, which means "son of a commandment," and is a mandatory rite of passage. The *Bar Mitzvah* boy pledges to obey the commandments given by God in the *Torah*.

I was eleven years old when my brother's *Bar Mitzvah* took place and it was an exciting event. Although generally shy in public, Stanley sang his portion of the *Torah* confidently and in perfect tune, and our parents were thrilled with his performance. Aunts, uncles, cousins, and dear family friends listened intently, pleased to be sharing in the *mitzvah,* the blessed event.

Although we were not especially well off at that time, my parents hosted a luncheon following the service at a rented facility downtown. A photo of the event shows the head table guests seated from left to right - mother's eldest sister, Molly Ratner, her brother Max, Abe Friedgut, Master of Ceremonies (standing), our father, Stanley, myself (although I cannot be seen because I am hidden by a lady with a big hat), Mother, Father's sister, Selma, Reverend and Mrs. Masters.

Abe, recently returned from three and a half years of overseas duty, was presently attached to the Canadian National Defense Headquarters in Ottawa. He was delighted to act as Master of Ceremonies. There were lots of speeches, including the traditional one from the *Bar Mitzvah* boy.

Stanley's Bar Mitzvah Speech

Montreal,
April 2, 1944

My dear parents, sister, relatives, and friends.

This is the greatest day in my life. I have been admitted into the Jewish fold, and am now on equal footing with all men in Israel. Until this day my father was responsible for all my deeds. Now I assume, in the eyes of Jewish Law and tradition, personal responsibility. I therefore make this pledge, that I shall do my best to grow up a good Jew and a good man.

I fully realize what I owe to my dear mother and father for all they have done and are doing for me. I am quite aware of the fact that I can never repay them for all their tender care, guidance and watchfulness over me. I also appreciate the debt I owe to my people, who for three thousand years have been struggling for survival. All I can say is that I shall try my utmost to deserve all this rich heritage, by making every just cause, my cause.

I also want to thank all of you for coming here this afternoon to take part in my rejoicing. I shall always look back upon this event as one of the milestones in my young life and will forever cherish the memory of everything that takes place in this room today.

Thank you.

As their first-born spoke, my parents rejoiced in the occasion. But as with all happy events, it was tinged with sadness too. In an immediate and deeply personal sense, they missed their family members who had passed away and could not share in this momentous event. Also in their thoughts were the millions of Jews in Europe who had perished, and were, at this very moment, still being brutally persecuted. In contrast, their lives were filled with immense pleasure as they gazed with pride at their son on the podium pledging allegiance to Judaism, and saw their young daughter's eyes fixed with pride on her older brother and his newly-acquired stature. They revelled in their own good fortune, which they would never take for granted.

Then it was Father's turn to speak and he seized the opportunity to discuss what he considered to be an appropriate topic for the occasion.

S. Bernard Haltrecht's Speech for his son Stanley's Bar Mitzvah

Montreal, April 2, 1944

As I sit here this afternoon and meditate, a number of thoughts pass through my mind, two of which, with your kind indulgence, I shall take the liberty of conveying to you.

I would like to discuss the relationship of parent to child. During the past three quarters of a century an effort has been made by many historians and economists to correlate all social events in terms of economic materialism.

There is, however, one outstanding item in life which does not seem to fit ito this picture, and that is the love, attachment and intense feeling of parents to children. What power is that which makes an otherwise weak and feeble woman the greatest of heroines when her efforts pertain to the welfare of her children? What power on earth gives a mother her Herculean strength to work day and night without let-up, and do the most arduous tasks so long as such effort is for the benefit of her children? What force is that which will, as if by magic, transform an otherwise stern man into a soft helpless being when his children are affected?

A man may be in his office, factory or business all day, meet the greatest of disappointments, go home a sick, tired and weary man. But as soon as his children meet him at the door, all his sorrows and tribulations disappear, as if by a magic wand. What is that power? It cannot be explained by the mere theory of economic materialism.

Students of biology tell us that it is the innate, instinctive struggle for survival that creates this apparently superhuman power. There may be truth in that, but certainly not all the truth. It is true that the struggle for survival is common to all life, animal as well as vegetable life. We notice, however, in the lower animals that the tenderness of the parent to its offspring is limited to the period only of helpless childhood. As soon as the child grows to maturity the parent turns it away, makes it shift for itself and pays no further attention to it.

Among humans a child remains a child to its parents, whether it is four or forty. The child may be separated from its parents by thousands of miles, and be absent and out of sight for many years; the attachment, however, does not cease. We must therefore supplement the theory of the struggle for survival by another additional theory.

My parents departed this life many years ago. They are non-existent to the rest of the world. To me, however, they have never died. They are living; they live within me. I see them before me all the time. I am the continuation of their existence on earth. In me, they have achieved immortality.

Similarly, when I look into the eyes of my children, I see my own immortality. They will continue my existence long after I shall have passed into the great and unknown beyond. It is in this phenomenon that we can unveil the true secret of the parents' intense feelings for their offspring. They are the flesh of our flesh, the blood of our blood, and the spirit of our spirit.

There is one other thought I should like to bring out this afternoon, and this one is particularly directed to my child, in answer to his opening remarks.

My son! You have pledged yourself this afternoon to do your best to grow up a good Jew and a good man. It is a great undertaking and a difficult one. It will require your very best, maybe more than your very best. Your effort, however, is not only an arduous duty. It is also a great privilege.

You have rightly remarked that for 3000 years our forefathers have been struggling for our survival as an ethnic unity. We must give an account of our stewardship. We must see whether we really deserve the great heritage which has been bequeathed to us and of which we are such proud heirs.

The existence, my boy, of the Jewish people as an entity in this and in past centuries is one of the great wonders of all time. The Jewish people have outlived many of the greatest and most powerful states. Take such powerful nations as the Chaldeans, the Assyrians, the Babylonians, the Egyptians, the Romans – where are they today? When we study about their mode of life we call it "ancient history."

The Jewish people, one of the smallest and one of the weakest in all history, still lives now, more virile and more numerous than ever. How can we explain that? If it were solely a question of physical strength we would have long ago passed into oblivion. What then?

Some maintain that the Jewish people have survived because we are a stubborn people, a stiff-necked people. There may be some truth in that, but only some, and not all of it. Look at Corinth and Cortage. There you have a stubborn people, a stiff-necked people. To their everlasting glory they died to a man in defence of their father-land, but where are the Corinthians and the Cartagenians today? No, my son, it is something more than stubbornness.

Many ascribe the Jewish survival to the universal persecution which we have undergone through the ages. The great Israel Zangwill in the beginning of this century came out with a cry of anguish appealing to all Christian peoples for tolerance to the Jews, declaring that if the Christian nations throughout the ages had treated the Jewish people in a Christian-like manner, there would not have been today one Jew in all Christendom. There may be some truth in that too, but certainly not the whole truth. Many races have been persecuted, and still they are nonexistent today.

Another school of thought tells us that the Jewish people have survived because we are the Chosen Race, selected by Providence for a special mission to teach all people righteousness. With all due respect to those who believe in this theory, I think it is only partially accountable for the survival of the Jew. We must bear in mind that nearly every nation considers itself to be the Chosen People.

You only have to listen every Sunday to Reverend Springett and his British Israel Society to see that many consider the Anglo-Saxon race the chosen people, the true descendants of the last tribes in Israel. The Germans, we know, to our great horror, are also convinced they are the master race, *das Herrenvolk*, the chosen people.

The Ethiopians are convinced that they are the chosen people and that their king is the King of Kings, a direct descendant of King Solomon. The Japanese claim to be a celestial race with their Emperor as a divine person, a direct descendant of the gods. Even the Red Indians consider themselves the only perfect people on earth, while the pale faced and colored people are imperfect productions by an inexperienced god. So you see, my son, we have to look somewhere else for the true meaning of our survival after 3000 years of struggle and twenty centuries of dispersion. What is it then?

I shall be quite frank. I agree with the philosopher Hegel. He maintained that a nation, a race, a people had the right to continued existence so long, and only so long, as it contributed to the welfare of all mankind. Once it has ceased to make such a contribution, it has forfeited the right to its existence.

The Jewish people during its long and tragic history, have without interruption or let up, constantly produced great men of vision, who contributed more than their proportionate share to the progress and advancement of the human race. Even in the days known as the Dark Ages, Jewish philosophers, thinkers, and mathematicians have contributed more than their share to help relieve the world's suffering and misery. Paradoxical as it may sound, in the beginning of the Renaissance when the Christian Church was losing its hold on its people through agnostic infiltrations, it was a Jew, Moses Maimonides, who saved the Church, with his work known as *Guide to the Perplexed*. Take a country like Germany, which has been so ungrateful to our people, where the Jewish population, at the zenith of its advancement, although only 1% of the general population, has produced more than 50% of its Nobel prize winners.

I maintain therefore, my son, that it is the constant and steady contribution of our people to the world at large that has fulfilled our existence. Your pledge this day to grow up a good Jew and a good man is more than a mere expression of words. It means that your example, your efforts, your behaviour will be a valuable contribution and may be a determining factor in the continued survival of our people. The generation to which you belong will decide whether the Jewish people shall continue to exist or not.

18 ✿ CELEBRATIONS

Mother was singing and swaying to "The Anniversary Waltz" and the air was filled with romance. On February 8th, 1946 it would be my parents' 25th anniversary and the stage was set. The invitations had been sent, the hall was booked, and now the doorbell kept ringing as silver gifts of all types were delivered to our house. Mother kept saying she was hoping for silver candlesticks to replace those stolen years ago from their house on St. Louis Square. I convinced Stanley this was a gift we should chip in and buy together. He agreed when I told him he would not have to go looking for it, I would take care of all that. I was 13 years old and knew how to shop.

We both had had bank accounts for years. When I had saved up my first dollar, Mother, ever the frugal one, showed me how to roll up the hundred pennies in cut-up brown paper. From that day on my savings and the family allowance cheques all went into my personal account at the Bank of Montreal on Van Horne and Rockland.

Now at 13, I felt not only independently wealthy, but I also travelled freely in the city. It was a freezing cold February day. I hated the cold weather, but this was an important mission. I pulled on my heavy lisle stockings, donned my Red River navy wool coat, and ran shivering all the way to the streetcar stop. I got off at St. Catherine Street and Union and crossed the busy street to Henry Birks jewellery store on St. Catherine Street where I found beautiful silver-plated candlesticks. I arranged for them to be delivered Saturday morning when I knew both mother and I would be at home.

Saturday morning, right on schedule, the doorbell rang. Mother, immaculately attired and properly corseted in one of her customary crisp housedresses, answered the door. The Birks deliveryman stood there holding a large box beautifully wrapped in silver paper tied with a blue satin ribbon. I could hardly contain my excitement. Mother carefully removed the pretty wrapping and opened the blue box contained within. "Silver candlesticks! Just what I wanted," she exclaimed. She opened the envelope containing the card. "The children! They're from the children!" She could not believe it. My usually low-key mother rushed to the telephone to reach her husband at his office. "The children bought us candlesticks," she exclaimed.

That evening, after dinner, with Stanley rushed off to Boy Scouts and I to Girl Guides, Father pulled up a kitchen stool to the sink so that Mother could sit comfortably while she washed the dishes. He helped by drying and putting the

STANLEY AND MURIEL

dishes away. She trusted him not to mix up the dairy and meat dishes and cutlery. They talked excitedly about the coming anniversary luncheon at the Tokay Restaurant.

Abe, who had been demobilized as a Major the year before, was now practising law in Toronto, and would be attending. Father had carefully prepared a program for the occasion and Abe, once again acting as Master of Ceremonies, would not be short of people to introduce. The assorted family talent was more than enough to fill an afternoon's entertainment.

PROGRAM

Hungarian Tokay, February 10, 1946

Mr. Abraham H. Friedgut, K.C., Master of Ceremonies

1. Wedding March … Miss Ida Ratner
2. "O Promise Me" sung by Mrs. Margot Pniewsky, accompanied by Miss Ida Ratner
3. Luncheon
4. S. Bernard Haltrecht introduces Abraham H.Friedgut as Master of Ceremonies
5. Opening remarks by Master of Ceremonies
6. Rev. M. Master ... Vocal Solo
7. Greetings by Mr. A.J. Livinson
8. Recitation by Miss Muriel Haltrecht
9. Greetings by Mr. Louis Glazer
10. Rev. M. Master … Vocal Solo
11. Remarks by Dora Haltrecht, the bride
12. "My Hero" from The Chocolate Soldier sung by Mrs. Margot Pniewsky accompanied Mr. Arnold Haltrecht. This song is by special request of the bride. "Ich Liebe dich" ditto.
13. Address by S. B. Haltrecht
14. Movies by Dr. Roman Pniewsky assisted by Messrs. Arnold and Albert Haltrecht
15. Concluding remarks by Master of Ceremonies.

As Number 8 on the program, I would present the monologue, "A Lesson with a Fan," by an unknown author. With the one required prop, I would perform this piece in its Comedy of Manners style.

If you wish to learn a lesson with a fan,
I am quite prepared to tell you all I can,
So ladies, everyone, pray observe how it is done,
This simple little lesson with a fan.

If you chance to be invited to a ball,
And you meet someone you don't expect at all,
And you want him close beside you,
While a dozen friends divide you,
Of course, it's most unladylike to call.

So you look at him a minute, nothing more,
When you cast your eyes demurely on the floor,
And wave your fan —— just so,
Well towards you, don't you know,
Oh! it's a delicate suggestion, nothing more.

When you see him coming towards you, simple you,
Oh! be very very careful what you do,
And with your fan just idly play,
and look down as if to say,
Oh! it's a matter of indifference to you.

Then you flutter and flutter with it so,
And hide your nose behind it so,
Until he begins to speak,
Then you just lay it on your cheek
In that fascinating manner that you all know.
And when he tells the old tale o'er and o'er,
And vows that he will love you evermore,
Gather up your little fan, and SECURE HIM, if you can,
Oh! it's a delicate suggestion, nothing more.

I had learned that poem at the Montreal Children's Theatre directed by two incredible ladies, Dorothy Davis and Violet Walters, with whom I had been taking drama classes since the age of eleven. My parents were thrilled with the choice of poem for their silver wedding anniversary. They considered it perfect for the occasion. It represented an era of courtship that in some ways mirrored their own. My mother nostalgically recalled how my father would politely ask, when they were out for a stroll, "May I take your ahm?" in the British accent he had acquired in London.

D. DAVIS

V. WALTERS

By the time Stanley and I arrived home, they had moved to the parlour where we caught them reminiscing. They were happy to have listening ears to repeat their story. Mother had been living in Montreal with her whole family, while Father lived alone, first out West in Saskatchewan, then in Kingston, Ontario. For eight years they courted mainly by correspondence, they said. These were the days, Father explained, before long-distance telephone came into frequent use, the days when courtship and correspondence were carried out in a formal manner, and even friends addressed each other by surname. They fondly recalled how they had known each other six years before addressing each other by their first names. "Those, of course, were the olden days," my brother and I retorted.

The day of the celebration, my mother, dressed in a blue silk dress with matching hat and veil, examined herself in her vanity table mirror. Mother was proud of her slim figure. When we would shop for clothes, she would nod in agreement with the salesladies who would turn to me and say, "Doesn't your mother have a nice figure for a mama of two?" Satisfied with her appearance, she nevertheless blushed with excitement when my father said, "Look at your mother. Isn't she a beautiful bride?" He held out his "ahm" for her to take, and the two of them stepped out of the house like bride and groom with us following close behind.

Before long their attention turned to the next family event. They had given a Bar Mitzvah in Stanley's honour, they had hosted a party to celebrate their silver anniversary, and next came their daughter's turn. My Sweet Sixteen a few years later was the most grand and frivolous of the family events. There were 100 invited guests in formal attire. There was a five-piece band. From my childhood my parents had noted that I was a social person with a large circle of friends. Though it may appear excessive to invite 100 guests to a Sweet Sixteen party, when broken down it becomes more comprehensible - 40 friends with dates and 20 close relatives.

Abe Friedgut would not be in attendance at this social event as he, his wife, Judith, and their three sons had just left to live in Israel.

But surprisingly, three cousins whom I never knew existed, a young husband and wife and her mother would be coming. They had arrived from Poland three weeks prior to the event. Who were these people? The mother was the half-sister of one of my father's nieces. Her stepmother, Masha, my father's sister, had perished in Poland along with her husband and seven of her 11 children. At my father's urging and with his help, three of the surviving children – Sam, Norman, and Regina – had emigrated to Montreal in 1929.

A second tragedy closer to home involved my British uncle Edmond. He was the professor of languages, married to aunt Anna, my father's sister. Three weeks before the Sweet Sixteen, uncle Edmond died in his sleep of a heart attack. Anna was distraught. My parents consulted the Rabbi about whether they should cancel the event. The Rabbi said that once plans had been finalized, the hall rented, the invitations sent, one should not cancel a *mitzvah*.

Anna and Edmond had no children, and now with her partner gone, aunt Anna could not abide the loneliness. Later she became a spiritualist and turned to Jesus. That phenomenon was to have later repercussions.

Unlike the former family events, my parents, not wanting to intrude on their daughter's privacy, kept a relatively low profile. There was no program of speeches or performances by family members. My parents ate their meal with the extended adult family at a separate rectangular table, and beamed with pride watching the youngsters mingling, laughing and dancing. Stanley, of course, brought a "date" and was part of the young people's group.

One of the most important issues of a Sweet Sixteen is the person one will invite to be her host. Since at the time I had a crush on a boy named Mark, I was delighted when he accepted the invitation to be host. After all, this would be the boy that I would kiss "on the lips" after blowing out the candles on the cake– in front of all my friends – but also in full view of my parents and all my relatives. What a challenge! And I survived, as had all my friends who also had major Sweet Sixteen parties.

The crush must have been mutual because Mark wrote two love poems for me. The best features of these verses were their adolescent sincerity and the solemnity with which they were presented. However, I cannot resist quoting the charming last two lines of one of the poems:

> She brings the sunshine and all that is well,
> And I love her truly, Dear Muriel.

19 ✿ TURNING POINTS

My parents had always shielded me from the persecution of the Jews in Europe. My rude awakening to the real meaning of the Holocaust came later when Father revealed my cousins' horrific background to me. I remember the occasion clearly. It was a brisk winter day. The new relatives had been living in Montreal for a couple of years. I was standing outside our house with my father, waiting for my mother and brother. My father mentioned that Sylvia, the recently emigrated Polish mother, would not be well enough to attend. When I asked what the problem was, my father replied, "After what she's been through, she is often not well." Of course, my curiosity was aroused, and I inquired about what she had "been through."

My father, who had always sheltered me, came right out and told me that the whole family had been in concentration camp, and that Sylvia's husband and son had been killed. Her 18-year-old son had been selected to build a crematorium with other strong young men. After it was built, the German officers used it to cremate these same young people. I could not believe my ears.

It seems incredible that I grew up not knowing about these atrocities. After the war, the Canadian Government permitted a number of European Jewish adolescents to emigrate to Canada, provided a family offered to care for them. I became friendly with two of these girls, Ella and Rosie, but they never discussed their painful experiences. Ella once did tell me she envied Canadian children who were so carefree and could laugh so easily. She said that after what she had seen, she found it difficult even to smile.

The author Helen Epstein, a daughter of survivors, writes that her mother used to say she "lost her laugh in the war." Ella did not elaborate about what she had seen, and I did not invade her privacy. While I knew about the war and that people had lost their lives, I did not have a graphic idea of the kinds of atrocities that had been committed. It was hard for me to imagine the extent of the Nazi's malice.

Meanwhile, the year before my Sweet Sixteen, a tragedy had occurred of which I was unaware; this was the death of my aunt Irene's son, Noah. In 1926 my father's sister, Irene, had married Leopold Teichner and moved to Germany. While on a visit to Israel in 1939, the German currency changed, leaving them without funds to return home. This serendipitous occurrence forced them to settle in Palestine where their four children, three girls, Batya, Miriam, and Tamar, and their son, Noah were born and grew up. Noah was 18 years old when he was killed in the 1948 war between Israel and the Arab States.

That same year, my love of theatre took me to Brae Manor Summer Theatre in Knowlton, Quebec. At first I was somewhat taken aback by the fact that I would be eating non-kosher food, and I pictured my mother's face when I reported on Brae Manor's cuisine. However, I adored bacon and eggs and whatever initial guilt I felt soon disappeared.

Vivid in my memory is the gentile ambience in which I was surrounded that summer. The signs on the Knowlton country club property where the theatre company went swimming read RESTRICTED CLIENTELE. We all knew what that meant - no Jews. I always felt a little uneasy. If they discovered that I was Jewish, would they send me away from their club?

That question was tested one Sunday afternoon. My parents had come from Montreal to see me perform in "Nine Pine Street," based on the true story of Lizzie Borden, accused of killing her

BATYA, TAMARA, NOAH, MIRIAM

parents ("gave her mother 40 whacks"). They stayed overnight at a nearby inn where I had reserved them a room. My mother later complained that it was situated by a mink farm and she couldn't sleep all night because of the smell. She also complained that I looked pale, was working too hard indoors, and was not getting enough fresh air.

I thought I would show her that there was a club nearby where I sometimes had a chance to relax and swim. On Sunday afternoon we went over to the Knowlton club with the others from Brae Manor. By this time my friend's father had arrived from Montreal and he joined the four of us on the lawn. He had an unmistakable Eastern European Jewish accent. Before long a club official took him aside, said it was a "private club," and suggested he leave. He reported this incident to my father who, with knowing looks, repeated it to us, and since it was time for the three of them to catch their train, they kissed us goodbye and quietly left.

The following year when, at 16, I entered Sir George Williams, the annual college winter carnival was being planned in Rawdon, a rural town in the Laurentian Mountains. When the student organizers of the carnival travelled to view the site, they noticed the RESTRICTED CLIENTELE sign. The bigotry of the sentiment was noted and the organizers brought back the news to the rest of the committee.

There were strong articles against it in *The Georgian*, the student newspaper. I was very moved and impressed to hear my gentile fellow students saying they were not going to visit any locale in which their Jewish friends were not welcome. The carnival was cancelled that year.

Another college controversy centred around the Hillel Foundation, which had been organized to represent the Jewish communities on campus. I discovered its existence from a poster announcing auditions for a production of *Trio*, an evening of three Jewish plays. I turned up and was cast in the role of Roma in "Winter" by Sholom Asch.

There was a radical young student at Sir George who wrote controversial articles in the student newspaper. His name was Mordecai Richler and he was very vocal in his opinions. He decided the Hillel Foundation should be abolished on the grounds that it was élitist. He wrote numerous articles expressing his point of view in his provocative manner. His views generated lots of discussion and arguments, but in the end, Hillel was preserved and exists to this day. Mordecai probably didn't much care, because he quit the College and left for London to write a novel. We had a good laugh over that one. Soon he was the one laughing when his novels, *The Acrobats* (1954) and *Son of a Smaller Hero* (1955) appeared in print.

Living in a flat on Ducharme with no accompanying garden in my younger years (by now we had moved to our own home with its own private garden) led our parents to believe their children were being deprived of scenic surroundings and country air. Father had joined the U.J.P.O. (United Jewish People's Order), and some of his comrades suggested he send us children to a camp sponsored by this organization. So off we went for three weeks of the summer months to Camp Kinderland at Fourteen Island Lake in the Laurentian Mountains, some 45 miles from Montreal. It turned out the children at the camp were mainly from homes east of Park Avenue and all were very familiar with the Yiddish language. Mornings we would assemble at the flag where often guest speakers would give lectures in Yiddish. Stanley now thinks they were trying to indoctrinate us in communist philosophy but since we understood nothing, their speeches had no effect.

Meanwhile, children our age in other parts of the world were not nearly as fortunate. In Britain, children from London had been torn away from their families and evacuated to rural areas where it was thought they would be safer from German bombs. Worse still, children in Eastern Europe were being sent to camps of an entirely different order.

Father's membership in U.J.P.O. took him out of the house one evening a week. This absence was very noticeable because my parents always socialized together. It was also noticeable because my mother was opposed to his attending this particular organization. Father insisted that it was "a sick benefit society" and although politics may have been discussed at the meetings, it was basically apolitical. Mother said it was "full of communists." One night my father came home with a gavel. He had been elected president of the society. She was not amused. This was a worry to me, and I remember having nightmares in which my father was chased by police and shot.

Eventually he gave up the society; it was forced to disband by the Quebec Padlock Law, which allowed the police to padlock any dwelling, even a private home, that was suspected of disseminating communist ideology.

Father always took a keen interest in history and politics and was extremely knowledgeable on these subjects. He was convinced this was the first time in Russia that a revolution had been created unselfishly for the benefit of the people. At last, the Russian people were not being betrayed. The masses had been held down for centuries under a series of czars but now under the new regime he believed that they were becoming educated; they were learning to read and write. My father believed that the Russians were an honest people and that they sincerely wanted to create a utopia in which the dichotomy of rich and poor would be eliminated and all would share equally in the wealth of the country.

Stanley, on the other hand, believed the reports that were filtering into the local newspapers, reports of terrorism and of massacres. Journalists reported that citizens with views differing from the government were being exiled to Siberia. Stanley was convinced that the new government was comprised of dictators just as corrupt as those that preceded them, while according to my father, the newspaper reports were strictly capitalist propaganda. But Stanley held his ground, maintaining his own political ideology. While Stanley was at university, my father concluded that his son had been influenced by his history and political science professors. To his credit, he said this kindly, without malice, more as one colleague about another whose views differed but who respected the other's perspectives.

In his university days Stanley belonged to a student Zionist group at McGill and their discussions and meetings fostered his desire to visit Israel. Stanley visited a kibbutz on the Lebanese border that had been formed jointly by Israelis and graduates of American universities in which earnings were shared equally by all members, whether they were cooks, farm workers, or cabinet ministers. This brand of socialism differed from its counterpart established in Russia where the goal was to have every citizen in the whole country share equally in the "wealth" (or perhaps the poverty, as it later turned out).

Before Stanley embarked on his trip, Father had made sure to give him Abe Friedgut's telephone number so that his lifelong friend and his son could meet, and he lived vicariously through every moment of Stanley's trip. Eyes shining with excitement, he would report to us each day, "Stanley is now in Tel Aviv, tomorrow he will be on the bus to Haifa," and so on throughout the six-week period. Stanley did telephone Abe, and was invited for a meal with Abe and Judith at their home. Abe talked at length about his close relationship with Bernard from 1914 in Regina when they had first met, and expressed regret that geography kept them so far apart.

On Stanley's return from Israel in 1953, the plane landed in New York so the passengers could change planes for Montreal. As he disembarked, two officers approached him and escorted him from the airport. He was being detained, they said, for being a communist. When he protested that he had never in his life belonged to any communist organization, that if anything, he was a Zionist, they were unimpressed. They took him to Ellis Island where he was detained overnight. The next morning he was served breakfast with hundreds of immigrants, many of whom had been detained for months. It was an educational experience that underlined his appreciation for his own fortunate circumstances. Later in the day, the officers admitted they had detained the wrong person and apologized. Perhaps the fact that he and my father have almost identical initials, S.B. and S.D., may have accounted for their error.

In the meantime, Dora and Bernard were awaiting news from Stanley. It had been arranged that he would telephone when he arrived safely in New York, but no news came. Father phoned the airline. Yes, the plane had landed, yes, his son had been on the plane. Next Father phoned the Agency. They were vague as to his son's whereabouts but they said they would look into it.

Due to the unforeseen detainment, Stanley arrived home a day later than expected. Our parents could not understand why he did not phone. He was unable to lie to them so he just said nothing, but my husband said that Stanley must have gone off with some cute girl that he met on the trip. The matter was dropped and we never revealed the true story.

When the American couple Ethel and Julius Rosenberg, parents of two young sons, were apprehended and accused of being communist traitors, my father, along with millions of others, believed that the two were innocent martyrs, not part of an alleged espionage team. He believed they were being attacked for their beliefs and not their actions, and the fact that they were Jewish didn't help.

One particular evening when my father's sister, Anna, was visiting, there was a conversation at the dinner table during which my father confessed his admiration for people who were brave enough to sacrifice themselves and their families for their deep beliefs. This dinner was aunt Anna's last visit to our house. Since her husband Edmond's death four years earlier, she had joined a spiritualist organization and had been informed that the centre of the movement was in New York. After having lived in Montreal for over 25 years she moved her life and belongings to the Empire Hotel, a small, elegant residential Manhattan hotel where she could be close to the people who shared her belief.

For a while we had cheerful letters from her about her new life and her involvement in spiritualism. Next came a letter giving a change of address. She had moved to a less elegant hotel to live more frugally. A couple of years later she wrote to say she had changed her living quarters yet again, this time to what appeared to be a rooming house.

Eventually my husband and I travelled to New York to visit her. We found her in a shabby rooming house near the railway tracks, most of her possessions gone. A framed photo of Christ adorned a side table. She said she remembered Him from when she lived in those early times. My once fashionable aunt had let herself go completely; her hair, now grey, was unkempt; her clothes, once impeccable, were slovenly; her dark brown eyes, once sparkling with life, bulged out of her gaunt face. It seems that her money and belongings, enough to support her for life, had been given to the spiritualist church to which she belonged. For some years now my father had been her sole financial support. Her sister, Selma, had disowned her because she had given up Judaism.

In 1954 my father received a telephone call from the New York police department. They informed him, as next of kin, that aunt Anna had died of a stroke and was lying in a Manhattan hospital. My father notified Selma's son, Leo, who lived in New York. Leo rushed to the hospital and viewed his aunt's body. Horrified to see that her neck was adorned with a cross, which she had taken to wearing since her "conversion," he ripped it off when no one was looking. Certain that over the last few years she had "gone off her rocker," he was determined to have her buried in a Jewish cemetery "where she belonged." Jewish cemetery officials would never accept a body wearing a cross. Thanks to her nephew and not without great difficulty, my aunt came to rest with her people, albeit in a strange country.

The previous June I had graduated with a BA, and two weeks later I married Maurice Gold. The year before that, when our engagement became official, my parents invited my future in-laws to our house for dinner. Dave Gold, who arrived in Canada from Russia in the 1920s, was thunderstruck when he saw my father. He immediately recognized and remembered him as the person who had welcomed and helped him settle 30 years ago when his feet touched Canadian soil. Like many immigrants who arrived in those days, he could never forget him. My father-in-law remained a staunch admirer of my father until the end of his life.

Before my marriage, I had been following in the Ratner family's tradition. To my mother's delight, I had been taking singing lessons. Mother revelled in the days when she and her sisters studied music with the eminent Alfred Laliberté and voice with Lucienne Boucher, his wife. Although Mother no longer sang at social functions, she constantly sang excerpts from light classical operas while she went about her duties in the house. And sometimes at informal house soirées with friends, she would be invited to sing. Father was especially proud of our mother who, he said, sang beautifully and received many compliments. At our family get-togethers, Ida, her younger sister, was always at the piano with us clustered around singing our favourite songs. From the time I could remember, our voices were characterized. Rebecca was a coloratura, Dora, a mezzo soprano, Annie was a contralto, and I was a lyric soprano.

The Diva in Action

PAULINE DONALDA

When I announced my readiness for singing lessons, my mother immediately recommended the renowned Pauline Donalda who had had a distinguished career in Europe and North America. She had sung with many of the famous opera singers of the day, including the illustrious Enrico Caruso. When she gave up her singing career, she returned to her family home in 1937 on Lincoln Avenue where she devoted herself to teaching and the founding and artistic directorship of the Montreal Opera Guild. My lessons were discontinued when I married.

Our two children were infants when I taught drama at The Montreal Children's Theatre two half days a week. When they entered elementary school I was engaged by the Protestant School Board of Greater Montreal as Drama Specialist to direct theatre productions. Designated as a program within the school curriculum, rehearsals took place within class hours. This meant I was on the same schedule as my children.

Teaching and directing theatre were rewarding, but I missed acting. Very few theatre groups existed in the city, and those that did exist rehearsed evenings, which would interfere with family life. My cousin Margot, the singer, belonged to ORT, (Organization for Educational Resources and Technical Training) a women's organization which, from time to time, invited guest artists to perform at their functions. She planted the idea in my mind. Would I come to their group and present a monologue? I mulled it over. Poring over possible presentations, I came across August Strindberg's *The Stronger*, acclaimed as "a jewel among monologues." In this dramatic piece a wife confronts her husband's former mistress.

The performance at ORT was well received, and largely through "word-of-mouth" I began to be invited by other groups to perform. Eventually I developed my one-woman show with a repertoire that included works by a variety of writers.

When Joyce Grenfell, the famous British comedic actress, was touring with her one-woman show, I found out in which Montreal hotel she was staying and wrote to her seeking advice. She graciously responded and invited me backstage following her show at Place des Arts. Her advice? "Write your own material, my dear." While I was considering her suggestion, I performed some more shows. Montreal playwrights began to attend my performances, which were now taking place in theatres. Four of these playwrights – Maxine Fleischman, Martin Bronstein, Marjorie Morris, and Betty Warshaw – wrote pieces for me that I eventually incorporated into my repertoire.

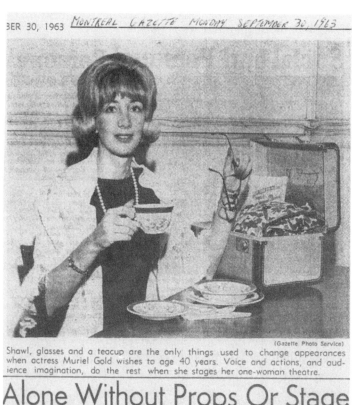

3ER 30, 1963 *MONTREAL GAZETTE MONDAY SEPTEMBER 30, 1963*

(Gazette Photo Service)

Shawl, glasses and a teacup are the only things used to change appearances when actress Muriel Gold wishes to age 40 years. Voice and actions, and audience imagination, do the rest when she stages her one-woman theatre.

Alone Without Props Or Stage
Actress Finds It A Challenge

My father died in 1962, so he was never able to see my one-woman show, which ran for nine years. During those years, my repertoire included plays by Bertolt Brecht (*The Jewish Wife*), Simone de Beauvoir (*The Woman Destroyed*) Ruth Draper (*Three Breakfasts, Doctors and Diets, Christmas Eve on the Embankment, A Southern Girl at a Dance*) and poems by Lawrence Ferlinghetti, Marion André, Jules Feiffer, and eventually readings of my own poetry and other dramatic readings. The following poem written during that period expresses the gratification I received from audiences.

ACTRESS

In the darkness
I crouch
taut   cold   ready to begin
tasting the cool presence of the anonymous unit

I rise   break ground

laughter leaps forward in flames
warming my body
- a cackling fire in a cold house -
each giggle sparking my flesh
each tear a hand touching me

This is the fuel that ignites my fire
makes the game real

I become all those women

20 ✡ GRANDFATHER'S WHITE HORSE

While Father lay dying in the hospital and the five of us were gathered round him, he had some requests. The first was that we look after our mother. "She's been a good mother," he began to say before my mother shushed him, embarrassed by the praise, or perhaps because she thought he was stating the obvious. Second, he requested that we all continue to get along with each other, and remain close, "not like some families." And about grieving he counselled, "Some tears I expect, but not too many."

The final request was addressed to Stanley and Sylvia, who had two daughters, Helaine and Maida. He requested that if they had a son in the future, they name him Noah after his famous great-grandfather. He added, "It is not mandatory," then repeated, "It is not mandatory," not wanting to impose his wish upon them. Two years later, on August 17th, 1964, Stanley and Sylvia had a son, and they carried out his late grandfather's wish. His Hebrew name was to be Noah, but they also wanted him named after our father, so he was to be known as Neil S. Bernard Haltrecht. On August eleventh, 1962, my revered father died. He was 69 years old.

Father was an intellectual, but above all, a humanitarian, a teacher, a social worker, and a mediator. He loved people. A former president of JIAS described him thus: "Mr. Haltrecht has a personality able to deal with the humblest and greatest of men." To the end of his days, no matter how overworked, harried or tired he was, when an engaged couple came to him for a marriage contract, they received for their $25, not just the required documents, but also a discussion of marriage, commitments, relationships and all sorts of helpful, non-intrusive advice. It was his pleasure to answer all their questions and address their concerns.

When Maurice, my first husband, became a C.A. (chartered accountant), my father arranged space for him in his suite of offices. Maurice would recount stories of how his father-in-law would spend an hour with an engaged couple paying $25 when a person with a more lucrative appointment (like Mr. Steinberg of the large grocery chain) waited in the reception room cooling his heels. Every client held equal importance in his estimation regardless of the size of their fee. That was the educator/social worker part of his personality. I once described this aspect of my father's personality to Irving Layton, our famous Canadian poet. He said, "You mean he was a human being." That was one way of putting it.

Mother, left on her own, put on a brave front. Independent in many ways, she had one fear, the lonely nights. She had never slept alone in an empty house, even when she was first married and my father was away on business trips for JIAS. She would cross the street and sleep at her family home. Now that her husband was gone, she did not want anyone else living with her, fussing around in her kitchen. Her sisters and brothers coaxed her to sleep at their house for the time being. She would have dinner with them, sleep there, and return home in the morning.

Meanwhile, to keep herself occupied, she enrolled in French classes in a school on Cote des Neiges, which catered to recent immigrants. She enjoyed being with the young people, and one day she asked one of the students if she would like to move into her house for a nominal rent – just to put it on a business-like basis. In return for this token payment, the girl's only responsibility would be to sleep in the house. This arrangement proved satisfactory and from then until the time of Mother's death in 1978, there was always a young female immigrant, generally from South America, living with her. These girls told me they liked the arrangement; they said it was like living with the grandmothers they had left back home. Two years following my father's death, Mother sold the house and moved into an apartment on Macdonald Avenue. I was helping her pack when I discovered the courtship letters.

The apartment was in close proximity to her four remaining siblings' home. Why did none of them marry? It would take a sociologist to explore the inner dynamics of the family to determine the cause. My father said that when he was courting my mother, the house was always filled with earnest young men interested in the sisters. It seems that the women never thought any of these men were either educated enough or sufficiently polished. Except for my mother and aunt Becky, their princes on white horses never arrived, and if they did, they were not recognized.

I recall that one Sunday at our home, during high tea, mother made an inadvertently tactless remark. Suddenly Annie burst out, "What do you know of my life? I was in love once with the most wonderful man, educated, kind, a true gentleman, but he was a gentile. Could I have married him and broken my parents' hearts?" There was a silence that came from a mixture of mostly astonishment and some compassion, after which the conversation shifted to safer topics.

Probably the saddest ending came to Rebecca, the aunt who had married her prince and moved to Los Angeles. In Montreal, she had been a librarian. She loved books, so when she eventually lost her eyesight, her husband, Henry Green, patiently read to her every evening, often from the Bible. A childless couple, they were devoted to, and dependent on, each other. When he died suddenly, it was as though she had lost not only a husband, but also her eyesight.

After her dear husband died, her sisters persuaded her to move to Montreal where they could look after her. When she began to fail, they cared for her until she became too ill to remain at home. Poor Rebecca ended up languishing in a chronic care hospital for several years. Always slight in build, she eventually shriveled to 78 pounds. But no matter how ill and disheartened she became, her music never left her. The songs that had filled her with joy in health now helped to sustain her in the dark days of her lengthy illness. Those around her could not help but feel inspired by the spirit that shone through the music emanating from her corner of the room. There she was, frail, blind, confined to her hospital bed and still singing in her frail coloratura voice.

After one of my visits to her, I wrote:

> She sits in another darkness/ her hair is white
> her eyes reach out from wrinkled skin
> searching for light
>
> She asks me the color of her hair
> I answer silver grey/ she smiles
> holds out her hand
> the veins jutting out like rivers
>
> Fingers print messages on my palm

I turn my head
She whispers of secret dangers
the muffled sounds remind me
of broken telephone games

She was probably the most erudite in the family and, being older than my mother and her remaining siblings, had a host of memories of the old country. Sometimes she would start to tell me about her early days in Russia, but it always seemed to tire her out. I would say, "When you will be feeling better, aunt Becky, I'll bring a tape recorder and you can tell me lots of stories."

But she never did improve in health and the stories are lost. Had I known I would eventually write a book about my family, I may have been more persistent. When I finally did embark upon the book, there was no one left to interview; my parents' generation, on both sides, was gone. I was forced to rely upon their letters, on written research and my own memories. I kept wishing I could rub a magic lamp and summon a genie to appear, so that I could ask for my one wish: that some of my ancestors, particularly my parents, might drop from the heavens for just as long as it would take to record their stories and fill in the missing pieces of this work.

Annie Ratner, the youngest of the eight Ratner siblings, was the last of the family to die. One day during a visit to her at the Town of Mount Royal nursing home when she recalled once again her "wonderful" life as a child, in her "wonderful" family, and the "wonderful" times they had, she mentioned her father's "beautiful white horse." This remembrance was news to me but for some reason, I didn't pursue it. But now, after all the extensive research, I am haunted by the recurring image of my grandfather's "white horse." In my efforts to reconstruct my family's history, what other parts of their lives have I missed out on? That horse has become a symbol of mystery, of the host of lost information that disappears with death, information that one can never regain.

And yet, I feel fortunate, for I have my parents' letters, which gave me more than a glimpse of their youthful personalities. There are those whose entire pasts have been annihilated, who have no letters, no photographs, no tangible objects, and only their own vague memories to sustain them. Perhaps worse still are those who have only bitter memories that burden their minds and impede their enjoyment of living. Compared to all these people, I feel fortunate indeed.

EPILOGUE

It is Sunday, a perfect autumn day in early September 2000. My daughter, Erica, her husband, Warren, and their two boys, Geoffrey, 12, and Kenneth, 10, have driven to Montreal from their home in London, Ontario, for Julien's *Bar Mitzvah*. Julien is Helaine's son, Stanley's and Sylvia's grandson. For this event I have given Julien, together with his *Bar Mitzvah* gift, a copy of his great-grandfather S.B. Haltrecht's speech to Stanley, at Stanley's *Bar Mitzvah* in 1944. The day I drop off the gift and the speech, Julien is home alone. "Your great-grandfather gave this speech to your grandfather, Stanley, at his Bar Mitzvah," I say. "I thought you might like to have it." He opens the folder, glances inside, looks up at me, and exclaims, "Wow! Thanks!" He kisses me and I leave.

That night his father, Michel, telephones. He says how touched they are by the speech and that he will quote some of my father's words when he delivers his "Father" speech at Julien's *Bar Mitzvah*. At the service, he incorporates the quote into his speech, and the audience, the Haltrecht family especially, is surprised and thrilled.

Kenneth has always wanted to see his Grandfather Maurice's grave. Maurice died of a heart attack in 1986, the year before Geoffrey was born. We decide that today is the day, and we all drive over to the Memorial Cemetery on de la Savane Boulevard. We are looking for The Hebrew Benevolent Society property of the Baron de Hirsch Institute, Section 63. After walking past the graves of many Montrealers, some once prominent members of the Jewish community, others lesser known, we find the three-and-a-half foot granite tombstone. The inscription on its base reads Maurice Gold, PhD.

GEOFFREY AND KENNETH

The boys notice some tombstones have pebbles on them, and they ask about them. None of us is sure of the origin of the Jewish tradition, but we tell them stones are placed on tombstones in remembrance of the dead. The boys solemnly place small stones on the tombstone. We stay and take photographs. They notice it is a double plot, with one half vacant, so I tell them the plot next to Maurice was reserved for me long ago. Someday, when I die, that is where I will be buried. When they ask about Grandpa Ron's plot, I tell them Grandpa Ron, as a scientist, wishes to donate his body to science. I see no need to discuss cremation with them at this moment, and we leave it at that.

Next we walk over to the Russian Polish property on the west side of the cemetery where their great grandparents, Bernard and Dora, are

155

GEOFFREY AND KENNETH

laid to rest side by side. Geoffrey runs ahead and spots it first. We all follow. Once again, the boys place stones on the tombstones, and I take photographs. To them it is a story, fiction, not real and vivid in their memories as it is for us. I tell them I am writing a book about their great grandparents so they and their children will know about their roots. "Cool," they say, "Can we go up to the mountain now? Let's hike up from Beaver Lake to the Chalet." It strikes me how fitting this outing is. Bernard and Dora walked and picnicked in the hills of Mount Royal all their lives. I look up at the clouds and think that somewhere they are both smiling down at us.

156

APPENDIX

Events Leading to the Lawsuit: Talk given by Bernard Haltrecht

I

"In September 1936 I decided to enter the studies leading to the notarial profession. I went to the office of the Board of Notaries for information and advice.

Mr. Courtois, the Secretary, received me courteously and gave me full information on the subject. On ascertaining that I hold the degree of Bachelor or Arts from Queen's University, he asked me to bring him the diploma as well as a certificate showing the subjects that I studied. He then outlined to me the methods by which one can eventually be admitted to the practice of the notarial profession.

He further pointed out that since the Board of Notaries meets only once a year, in the month of July, I could not be officially admitted to the study until the summer of 1937. But if I obliged myself to a notary at once, and filed a copy of my indenture with the office of the Board, I could (on payment of $100.00) have a by-law adopted to count my studentship as from the date of the filing of the copy.

I then wrote to the Registrar of Queen's University, and within the course of a few days received a certificate of my studies that I left with Mr. Courtois, I also left with him my diploma. Mr. Courtois then told me that my next step was to get indentured and have a copy registered with the Board.

Accordingly, on September 22, 1936 I obliged myself as articled clerk to Mr. Benjamin A. Schwartz, Notary Public. The same day, on the payment of $3, I had a copy of my indenture filed and registered in the office of the Board of Notaries.

On September 24, I registered with the McGill University Law Faculty as first student at law. Thus, during the winter of 1936-37 I was occupied with the studies at McGill and attended at the office of Mr. Schwartz in accordance with the terms of my indenture.

II

In May 1937 after completing my first year's law studies, I went to the office of the Board of Notaries to notify them of my change of address (from Davaar Avenue, Outremont, to Hingston Avenue in Notre Dame de Grace). I was handed two forms: one, an identification certificate form, to be filled in and signed by a responsible university official to the effect that I am the holder of the degree of Bachelor of Arts. The other contained information for prospective students, as well as an outline of a form notifying the Secretary of the Board of one's intention to apply for the admission to study.

I took these two forms to the Dean of the Law Faculty of McGill University who filled in the identification form and also certified my signature on the other form.

The next day I took both these forms to the office of the Board of Notaries. Mr. Courtois, on looking them over, said that whereas I am a graduate of Queen's University, it is essential that I have similar forms certified by that institution.

Within the course of about ten days I received the required identification certificate from Queen's properly completed. My signature was also certified by the Vice-Principal of the University. I presented these to Mr. Courtois, who examined them closely, and asked me what other documents I had to identify myself. I, in turn, inquired as to what documents he would like me to produce.

I told him that I had an official graduation year book where he could find both my photograph as well as a write-up. He said this was not what he wanted. I then suggested that a number of prominent men in the city of Montreal could identify me in person.

He then took out from his file the certificate of studies that I had left with him last September, looked at it closely, and said, "I don't see any philosophy." I walked over to his chair and pointed to a course in Mental Philosophy. Mr. Courtois said, "That's right," and apologized for overlooking it. He then asked me whether I had my naturalization certificate. I said, "Yes" and produced it. He examined it and asked permission to keep it in his file. Finally he asked me, "Do you have your birth certificate?"

This conversation took place on Friday morning June 11. I explained to Mr. Courtois that I was born in a distant land, in Poland. I left it as a small boy, when it was part of the Old Russian Empire. Since then that country had undergone a world war, a civil war and a revolution. I heard that during the wars and revolution fighting took place in the streets of the very town where I was born. I was therefore not quite sure whether my records were still in existence. If they were, I could get them; it was only a question of time.

Mr. Courtois said that my documents would have to be complete in his hands 15 days prior to the meeting of the Board, namely by June 28. I said I was somewhat doubtful that I could produce the required certificate within such a short time, but I would try my best. Mr. Courtois regretted that he had to put me to all this trouble but, he said, the law required it. He wanted to make sure that once my application was presented at Quebec, there should be nothing missing and I should have no further difficulties.

I thanked him for his courtesy and before leaving I wished to know if there would be anything else required of me should I be able to produce the birth certificate. Mr. Courtois said he did not think so, except that I should have to pay the usual fee. I offered to pay the fee immediately, but Mr. Courtois could not as yet accept it.

I then proceeded to the office of the Polish consulate on Stanley Street. I told the Secretary that I needed a birth certificate from his country. He told me that since I am a British subject, I would have to apply to the British authorities to get it for me. He advised me to write to the British Consulate in Warsaw, where in turn they would write to the town council of my place of birth, and in due time I should get the certificate.

I explained to the Secretary that this would be a slow process, while he could communicate by cable directly with the town hall of my birthplace and within a few days I could have a cabled reply as to whether or not my records are there. If they are found, a birth certificate could be dispatched by airmail, and I could probably have it within two weeks. The Secretary went into the private office of the Consul General and in a few minutes returned saying he was sorry, that since I was not a Polish citizen, I was not under their jurisdiction and they could do nothing for me.

I demanded to see the Consul General in person. I told the latter I realized I had no claim on Polish authorities. This, however, was a very urgent matter for me and I asked him to do it as a special favour. He looked puzzled as to why I came to him at such a late date, but he finally consented. I asked him to send a cable with a prepaid reply. If my records were found, they should rush them by airmail.

He said, "A cable to Poland, a cabled reply air mail, birth certificate, consular fees; it is going to cost you a lot of money." "True," I said, "I can ill afford this expense. But I must have the certificate at all costs. If it arrived a little late, I would at least have the official cable from your government, which I hope will satisfy the Board of Notaries."

On the afternoon of Monday, June 14, the Polish Consulate advised me by telephone that a cable was received to the effect that my records were located, and that my birth certificate was being forwarded by mail. The next morning June 15, I called for the cable, had it translated, and the translation officially certified by a commissioner. On the 16th I presented the original cable to Mr. Courtois, who looked them over and was satisfied. I was now at liberty to make the official application for the admission to study.

On Friday June 19th I deposited with the office of the Board a cheque for $230 to cover $130 fee for the admission to study, and $100 for the by-law to count my studentship as from September 22, 1936.

On Tuesday June 22nd, the office of the Polish Consulate informed me that the birth certificate had arrived. When I called the next morning I had to comply with certain formalities and since Thursday June 24th was a legal holiday, I procured the certificate on Friday, June 25. I had it translated into English, and on Saturday morning the translation was certified by a Notary Public. At ten o'clock Monday June 28 I presented the original certificate, with the certified translation to Mr. Courtois.

III

On the evening of Tuesday July 13 I received a telegram from Mr. Courtois from Quebec to the effect that the Board had rejected my application due to lack of a required philosophy course. If I desired to present any arguments I could come to Quebec, since the Board would be in session Wednesday and Thursday.

On Wednesday evening I called on Mr. Peter Bercovitch [a prominent Montreal lawyer] and showed him the telegram. He advised me to go to Quebec to give the Board any explanations they may demand of me. I consequently wired Mr. Courtois that I was coming, and took the midnight train to Quebec.

On Thursday morning at 8:30 I phoned Mr. Courtois to his room at the Chateau Frontenac. He informed me that the Board held its sessions at the Court House and that I should be there at 9:45.

At 9:30 I was at the Court House. As the various members appeared I noticed that the only other member besides Mr. Courtois that I knew was Mr. George Marler. Mr.

Marler greeted me in a very friendly manner and expressed to me the hope that my application would be successful. It was Mr. Marler who during that entire day kept me informed of the progress of my case.

I sat in the hall from 9:30 till noon, when the meeting adjourned for lunch. Mr. Marler advised me that my case had been handed over to a special committee, who would deliberate on it in the afternoon. I should therefore be back by 2:30 p.m.

At 2:15 I was back. I was waiting in the hall till 5:00, when the committee adjourned. Mr. Marler informed me that the committee split four to four, and that their report would be submitted to the full meeting of the Board at the evening session. It was therefore advisable for me to be back at 8.00.

At eight o'clock I returned to the Court House. I was again waiting in the hall for results till 11:30. The meeting adjourned, the members of the Board filed out of the room, and Mr. Marler, in a sad and disappointed voice, informed me that my appeal had been dismissed. I just had enough time to take a taxi and rush to the station to catch the 11:55 train for Montreal.

IV. Concluding Remarks.
In reviewing this case, three angles present themselves:
1. The Personal Angle.
2. The National Angle.
3. The Racial Angle

1. Personal.   Had I known last September of the difficulties that were to confront me in connection with my rights to the study for the notarial profession, I doubt whether I would have ventured out for this undertaking. It is for me, to say the least, extremely painful to have to bring to court the very people with whom I would have liked to be on the best of terms, and on whom I had hoped and still hope to be able to look upon as my leaders, and to count on for advice and guidance.

But alas! I have gone too far to be able to retrace my footsteps. I have practically given up my business, and devoted a whole academic year to the study of law. I have invested a great deal of money, time and energy. I have now no choice, but to go forward with my plans, regardless of obstacles.

2. National.   However important the personal element may be, there is in this case a far greater principle involved. It seems more than a coincidence that the two rejected applicants are both graduates of English-language Universities. I fully appreciate the jealousy with which our French-speaking fellow citizens guard the culture of the forbears.

3. Racial (Pages are missing)

SELECTED BIBLIOGRAPHY

Baltzan, Jacob A. *Memoirs of a Pioneer Farmer in Western Canada at the Dawn of the Twentieth Century.* (First published as articles in the *Israelite Press*, Winnipeg, Manitoba, 1936-1937.) Toronto, 1994.

Barnhart, Gordon L. *Peace, Progress and Prosperity: A Biography of the Hon. Walter Scott* (Doctoral Thesis). Saskatoon: University of Saskatchewan, 1998.

Bermant, Chaim. *Point of Arrival: A Study of London's East End.* London: Eyre Methuen, 1971.

Bibbing, Winnifred Theresa. *"An English School Marm in Saskatchewan."* Saskatoon: Saskatchewan Archives, 1912. (Unpublished letters, call no. S-A160.)

Campbell, Eleanor. *Reflections of light: a History of The Saskatoon Normal School (1912-1953) and the Saskatoon Teacher's College (1953-1964).* Saskatoon: College of Education, University of Saskatchewan, 1996.

Cohen, Israel. *Vilna.* Philadelphia: The Jewish Publication Society, 1992.

Collard, E.A. *Montreal: The Days That Are No More.* Toronto: Doubleday & Co., 1976.

Cooper, John I. *Montreal: The Story of Three Hundred Years.* Montreal: Imprimerie De Lamirande, 1942.

Currie, A.W. A. "The Grand Trunk Railway of Canada, 1957." *Canadian Encyclopedia,* pp. 764. Edmonton: Hurtig Publishers Ltd., 1985.

Deslisle, Esther. *The Traitor and the Jew. Anti-Semitism and Extremist Right-Wing Nationalism in Quebec from 1929-1939.* Translated by Madeleine Hébert with Claire Rothman and Kathe Roth. Montreal: Robert Davies Publishing, 1993.

Donalda, Pauline. "A Jewish Singer's Career: Impressions by Pauline Donalda." *Canadian Jewish Year Book* (1940-41), Vol. II.

Dyboski, Roman. *Poland.* London: Ernest Benn Ltd., 1933.

Figler, Bernard, Q.C. "Biography of Louis Fitch, Q.C." *Canadian Jewish Profiles.* File no. 12330, Serial no. 200281. Copyright by the author, Ottawa, Canada 1968.

Gubbay, Aline. *A Street Called The Main.* Montreal: Meridian Press, 1990.

Hart, Daniel, ed. *The Jew in Canada*. Montreal: Jewish Publications Limited, 1926.

Hustak, Alan. "St. Louis Square." *The Montreal Gazette* (June 16, 1996). p. C1.

Katz, Ephraim. *The Film Encyclopedia*. New York: Thomas Cromwell Company, 1979.

Jenkins, Kathleen. *Montreal: Island City of the St. Lawrence*. New York: Doubleday and Company, Inc., 1966.

Jones, Donald. "Cupar (Saskatchewan), 1905." *Pioneer Portraits, 1905-1965*. Cupar: Saskatchewan Archives, 1965. (Mimeographed unpublished history, call no. S-F157.)

Kirshner, Sheldon. "Vilnius Has Rich Jewish Past." *Canadian Jewish News* (January 7, 1993).

Knott, Leonard L. *Montreal 1900-1930*. Toronto: Nelson, Foster and Scott, 1976.

Lasnier, Rina. "Alfred Laliberté, homme libre. " *Les Carnets Victoriens*, XIVe annee, No. 3 (juillet 1949), pp. 207-213.

Martz, Fraidie. *Open Your Hearts: The Story of the Jewish War Orphans in Canada*. Montreal: Vehicule Press, 1996.

Meyer, Marion E. *The Jews of Kingston*. Kingston: Limestone Press, 1983.

"Weather Man Fickle as Woman," *The Montreal Daily Star* (March 6, 1920)

Neilson, Helen R. *Macdonald College of McGill University 1907-1988: A Profile of a Campus*. Montreal: Corona Publishers, 1989.

Paris, Erna. *Jews, An Account of Their Experience in Canada*. Toronto: Macmillan of Canada, 1980.

Penfold, George E. "Some Impressions." *Pioneer Portraits, 1905-1965* Cupar: Saskatchewan Archives, 1965. (Mimeographed unpublished history, call no. 5F157.)

Potok, Chaim. *The Gates of November: Chronicles of the Slepak Family*. New York: Ballantine Books, 1996.

Richardson, Joanne. *Sarah Bernhardt and Her World*. London: Wiedenfeld and Nicolson, 1977.

Richie, Alexandra. *Faust's Metropolis: A History of Berlin*. New York: Carroll and Graf Publishers, Inc., 1998.

Rinfret, Fernand. "M. Alfred Laliberté: Pianiste et Compositeur." *La Revue Moderne* (15 avril 1920), pp. 12-14.

Sir George Williams College Year Book, Retro '53. Montreal: Sir George Williams College.

Ship, Dave. "Norman Massey, 1908-1995." *Articles by Norman Massey.* Montreal: unpublished, 1994.

Snell, John Ferguson. *Macdonald College of McGill: A History from 1904-1955*. Montreal: McGill University Press, 1963.

Weintraub, William. *City Unique.: Montreal Days and Nights in the 1940s and '50s.* Toronto: McClelland & Stewart, 1996.
:

INDEX

About
the
Author

Muriel Gold

Muriel Gold, theatre educator, producer/director, grew up in Montreal, attended Strathcona Academy, received her B.A. from Sir George Williams, her M.A. from McGill, and her Ph.D. from Concordia. She is former Artistic Director of the Saidye Bronfman Centre Theatre, for which, during her eight-year tenure, she won acclaim from theatre critics, academics and the public at large.

For ten years she was on the McGill faculty where she taught acting. At Concordia, she taught Drama in Education and Drama with Special Populations. From1995-2000 she taught and guest-directed in the Professional Theatre Department at Dawson College. She has given workshops for the PSBGM to drama teachers. For the past six years, she has been giving workshops to the graduate Drama Therapy students at Concordia University that culminate in collective creation presentations. She has given workshops and lectures in Canada and the U.S. At Place des Arts she directed "Fineman's Dictionary," by Samuel Gesser. It starred Fyvush Finkel and Linda Sorensen.

Dr. Gold is the author of several other books:

The Fictional Family - in Drama, Education and Groupwork. Springfield, Illinois: C.C. Thomas, 1991.

Therapy through Drama: The Fictional Family. Springfield, Illinois: C.C. Thomas, 2000.

Drama across the Curriculum: The Fictional Family in Practice.

A Gift to their Mother: The History of the Saidye Bronfman Centre Theatre. Work in Progress.